Love and Revolution

The first 101 years of the automobile

By Richard A. Wright

Love and Revolution:
101 Years of the Automobile
By Richard A. Wright
Illustrated by Hank Van Fleteren

Published by Thirty-Three Publishing
Division of Spelman Productions, Inc.
Box 3333
Farmington Hills, MI 48333-3333

Copyright © 1988, The Detroit News and Thirty-Three Publishing Division, Spelman Productions, Inc.
Printed in the United States of America

ISBN: 0-933803-08-7 Softcover.
Library of Congress Catalog Card Number: 87-050743.

Acknowledgements

We wish to acknowledge the invaluable help of a number of people in the gathering of information for this book, including: Stan Drall and Ray Windecker, Ford Motor Co.; Dave Crippen, The Henry Ford Museum; Tom Jakobowski, Tom Houston, Moon Mullins, Ann Lalas, John McCandless and Lee Sechler, Chrysler Corp.; Ed Lechtsin, Nancy Libby, Ralph Kramer, Marlene Marlowe, Richard Thompson, John Mueller, Norb Bartos, Helen Early Jones, Phil Workman and Cliff Merriot, General Motors; Ben Dunn, American Motors; Al Rothenberg, Gene McKinny and Jim Wren, Motor Vehicle Manufacturers Association; Dr. Donald Softly, Detroit Historical Museum; Dean Kruse, classic car auctioneer, Auburn, Ind.; Jack Miller, Ypsilanti, Mich., the world's last Hudson dealer; George Crocker, president of the Rear View Mirror, Nag's Head, N.C., and partner in Tom Monaghan's Domino's Pizza classic car collection, Ann Arbor; George Levy and Jim Sawyer, AutoWeek magazine; Grace Wilson, Automotive News; Bob Lienert, formerly of Automotive News; Joe Molina and Pamela Spencer, JMPR; the staff of the Detroit Public Library main branch and the staff of the Detroit News reference library.

Love and Revolution

The first 101 years of the automobile

By Richard A. Wright
Illustrated by Hank Van Fleteren

Contents:

Clockwise, from top:
Mercedes Jellinek;
Gottleib Daimler; Barney
Oldfield and Ty Cobb in an
early Benz; Karl Benz

In the beginning: Daimler and Benz

It could be argued that since the development of agriculture about 12,000 years ago, the invention which has had the most profound effect on the way we live has been the automobile.

There have been many advances in technology which have had important and far-reaching effects, but few have changed the way we actually live as completely and as rapidly as the automobile.

We reserve for the car an emotional relationship we do not have with other machines, such as refrigerators, or airplanes or even the curiously human computer. The car has been venerated as an object of affection, excitement, even love. And when it fails us, we heap upon it the bitterness and intense anger we generally reserve for our loved ones.

Think for a moment about the world of 100 years ago. Travel was slow and difficult. A trip to anywhere was a major undertaking. Dearborn was a day's journey from Detroit on the road to Chicago. Most roads were just gravel or dirt.

Cities, usually built on streams or lakes or rail lines were compact and congested. They were quickly transformed by the car into sprawling urban complexes, held together — and in some ways split apart — by the freeways and interstates that bind them.

Buildings have been razed and farmland paved over to provide parking for the almost 300 million vehicles we own in the United States alone.

And along those roads are motels (motor hotels), fast-food restaurants, shopping malls, drive-in movies, drive-in banks, drive-in florists, even drive-in funeral homes.

In this century, the auto has spawned whole industries where none were before. Depending on whose figures you accept, one in six or one in seven working Americans is engaged in the building, selling or maintenance of motor vehicles. The Census Bureau says auto dealerships account for 28.5 percent of all the retail business in the United States.

Auto makers are the biggest or among the biggest consumers of steel, aluminum, copper, glass, zinc, leather, plastic and platinum and they use most of the lead and rubber consumed in the United States.

The automobile is not cheap. In addition to its voracious consumption of resources at the societal level and our income at the personal level, its toll of death and injury easily surpasses war many times over. Auto accidents are the leading cause of death of Americans from age 5 to 45.

But there is no talk or banning the auto or even seriously restricting it. Most of us consider a driver's license a right, not a license. Controversy rages over such "invasions" of our rights as laws requiring use of safety belts and 55-mph speed limits. In Germany, in fact, a bitter battle has been raging for some time over the imposition of *any* speed limit on the autobahns.

The automobile is, like no other machine, part of us.

The automobile's time had come 101 years ago, but it wasn't here yet. Here and there around the world, men were at work on motorized vehicles, unknown to each other, separated in time and space the way we are now from other planets.

Karl Benz and Gottlieb Daimler in Germany; Louis Renault, Rene Panhard, Emile Lavassor and the Peugeot brothers in France, and in the United States, Frank and Charles Duryea, Ransom E. Olds, Charles King, Elwood Haynes, David Buick and Henry Ford — all were working on vehicles they called by various names. For the most part, they worked in ignorance of each other.

Benz in Germany was the first to put an automobile into production, a three-wheeler he built in 1885. Just when his first delivery took place is not clear. It could have been late 1885. It seems more likely that it took place in spring of 1886. In the United States there were tinkerers, but no industry until 1895.

In fact, when Benz first got his three-wheeler chugging into movement in Mannheim, it was not the first time a vehicle had propelled itself. What was new was that Benz perfected his machine, put it into production and people bought it.

Isolated instances of automotive promise had come and gone. As early as 1769, Nicolas Cugnot fitted a wagon with a steam engine, fired it up and ran it across a field in France, thereby becoming, as far as we know, the first person to make and operate a powered vehicle. Incidentally, Cugnot's machine did not handle well and he ran it into a wall, the world's first auto accident. Legend has it he was arrested for his trouble and so might also be credited with the world's first moving violation.

The first internal combustion engine was built in 1860 by Ettienne Lenoir in France, but it ran on illuminating gas and was quite different from the modern engine. But in 1876, Nikolous Otto patented the four-stroke gasoline engine — the type used today — in Germany.

Benz's first automobile had a mid-mounted engine (currently very trendy in sports-car circles) with semi-elliptical leaf-spring suspension in the rear and none in the front. It had a tiller for steering. The engine was a 1.7-liter (about the size of the base engine in the Omni and Horizon) one-cylinder unit which put out 1.5 horsepower.

Meanwhile, in Cannstaedt, near Stuttgart, Gottlieb Daimler was working on a four-wheel, gasoline-powered automobile, which he had running in 1886. By 1888, he had begun talking with William Steinway, of piano fame, about licensing his car for manufacture in the United States. (Like almost all current automotive trends — Volkswagen, Nissan and Honda are assembling cars in this country and Toyota and Mazda are planning to — it's been done before.)

Daimler also got involved in an English Daimler operation and served as a director until 1898, but the British and German Daimler firms went their own ways.

A flamboyant Austrian businessman named Emil Jellinek, who was Austro-Hungarian vice-consul in Nice, France, had bought a special Daimler racing car in 1897 and in 1900 joined the Daimler board of directors, where he urged a new approach to auto design. Jellinek wanted cars to be longer, lower, lighter and faster.

Daimler's engineers were at work on such a car and Jellinek said he would buy the first 36 himself to sell in France, provided his distributorship territory was expanded and that the car with the three-pointed star insignia be named after his 10-year-old daughter, Mercedes.

In 1926, the Daimler and Benz companies merged and Mercedes became Mercedes-Benz.

Frank Duryea

Arthur W. White

Charles B. King

MOTOCYCLE RACE
2ND PRIZE
CHICAGO NOV. 28-95

5

22

American industry is born in the snow of Chicago

It did not look promising.

The Great Chicago Auto Race of 1895 had all the earmarks of a fiasco. It had already been delayed twice and when it finally started on Nov. 28, 1895, there was snow on the ground.

A snow plow (pulled by a team of horses, of course,) was brought in to clear the starting area. There were disappointingly few entries and most of them were European, German-built Benz cars. Boys pelted the vehicles — popularly called "motocycles" then — with snowballs.

But the race went on and, when it was over, an American car had beaten the best from Europe. (Cars had been in production in Europe for 10 years. No cars were yet in commercial production in the United States.) More importantly, perhaps, it had beaten the horse.

The American auto industry was born. But it was an unlikely beginning.

Herman H. Kohlstaat, who had made a fortune in the bakery business, took his public service responsibilities as publisher of the Chicago Times-Herald seriously and decided to drum up interest in the automobile (not yet called that), which was becoming all the rage in Europe.

He announced early in 1895 that his newspaper would sponsor the first race in the United States for horseless carriages, offering $5,000 in prizes, including $2,000 for the winner. Within a month, Kohlstaat uncovered a startling fact — the newspaper received 60 letters and telegrams from people who wanted to enter a car in the race. Some of these automobiles were imported from Europe, but a surprising number of them were being built by their owners.

The publisher had discovered that there was a widespread effort in the United States to build automobiles and that most of these inventors were not aware of the work of others, either here or in Europe.

Many said they wanted to enter their cars in the race, but would not have them ready by Labor Day, which was the date Kohlstaat had in mind. Since he wanted as many entries as possible, he delayed the race until Nov. 2.

Excitement mounted. When the big day arrived, 80 automobiles had been entered. Two showed up.

The only contestants on Nov. 2 were Frank Duryea, of Springfield, Mass., in a car he built based on designs by his brother, Charles, and Oscar Mueller in a German-built Benz owned by his father, a machine shop operator in Decatur, Ill.

Most of the other 80 entrants urged Kohlstaat to delay the race one more time, until Thanksgiving Day, Nov. 28. Kohlstaat was in a difficult position. A race with only two contestants seemed a bit ridiculous and rival newspapers, sensing a possible humiliation, were already picking up the scent. The Times-Herald had hyped the event and there would be spectators waiting to see a race.

So Kohlstaat talked to Duryea and Mueller and they agreed to stage an exhibition for the spectators. The actual race would be delayed one more time to Nov. 28, Thanksgiving Day. The exhibition was to run from Jackson Park to Waukegan and back, 90 miles roundtrip.

Frank and Charles Duryea quickly pulled ahead of Mueller's Benz, but their car frightened a team of horses at a crossroad near Evanston. The team bolted onto the road into the Duryea's path. Frank, who was driving, ran into a ditch to avoid hitting the wagon and smashed the car's differential housing.

The car was pulled back to the railroad station by a horse and transported back to Springfield for repairs before the big race. The Mueller Benz won the exhibition, but the horse was still champion.

Thanksgiving Day, Chicago was covered with four to six inches of snow. Several cars entered in the race either broke down or were unable to get through the snow to the starting line. But the race, looking more and more like a disaster, finally got under way.

Six cars started. Two were electrics, which quickly ran out of power. So the race — shortened because of the snow to a 55-mile run to Evanston and back —

pitted the Duryea against three Benz "motocycles."

One Benz was Mueller's. Another had been entered by the R.H. Macy store of New York, which was importing German-built Benz cars and hoped to sell them in Chicago as a result of publicity from the race. The other was entered by the De LaVergne Refrigeration Co. of New York.

Outside Chicago, the Duryea passed the Macy Benz, which later collided with a hack and did not finish. On the way back from Evanston, Duryea passed the Mueller Benz, then overtook the De LaVergne Benz. The Duryea crossed the finish line with no other car in sight. An hour and a half later, the Mueller Benz appeared, the only other car to finish the race.

The Duryea had beaten the three German cars, but perhaps even more importantly, it had made clear the days of the horse as the prime mode of transportation were numbered. No team of horses could have done what the Duryea did.

Each car carried an umpire and one of the umpires, assigned to Mueller's car, was Charles B. King, the first man to operate a car in Detroit, who had hoped to enter his own car in the race, but did not have it ready. King, incidentally, did get to drive in the race because Oscar Mueller, apparently overcome by fatigue and excitement, had passed out during the race and King drove the car to the finish line.

The Duryeas built their car in Springfield, Mass., but the American car is a creature of the Midwest (as were the Duryeas — they originally came from Illinois). With a few notable exceptions, most of the early automotive pioneers were from the Midwest and Great Lakes area.

In fact, the industry very nearly was located in New England. After his success in the Chicago race, Frank Duryea returned to Massachusetts and began building the Duryea car. In 1896, Duryea was the biggest producer in the United States, turning out 13 units. The cars were hand-built. Mass production of machines as complicated as an automobile was still years away.

The reason for the Duryeas' success where so many others failed was the efficient two-cylinder, four-cycle internal-combustion engine which powered it.

New England had one more shot at becoming the motor capital before Detroit took that title. Col. Albert Pope, who had served on Gen. Ulysses S. Grant's staff during the Civil War, converted his bicycle plant in Hartford, Conn., to automobile manufacture with the help of Hiram Percy Maxim. After their victory in Chicago, the Duryeas considered having Pope build their car, but Pope was not very interested. He did not think the internal-combustion engine could compete with steam or electric power.

While his plant did build a few gasoline-powered cars, its production heavily favored steam and electric. By 1899, Pope was the biggest manufacturer in the country, with output of 2,092 vehicles, almost half of the cars built in the United States that year.

But Pope had bet on the wrong horse. While steamers and electrics hung on as late as the '30s, they began losing out to the gasoline engine not long after the new century got under way.

In Lansing, Olds had built his first steam-powered auto in 1886. He switched to internal combustion, thinking it the most promising powerplant, and he entered the Chicago race, but did not have a car ready in time that he thought would be good enough to compete with the Benz models from Europe. He did not even know about the Duryea.

When Olds became the first to mass-produce autos, he powered them with internal-combustion engines. So did Henry Ford when he showed the world what mass production really was all about. The Stanleys and Dobles built some magnificent classic steamers into the '30s and electrics were still favored by a few Grosse Pointe dowagers into the '40s. But it soon became clear that the automotive mainstream would be dominated by the internal-combustion gasoline engine.

Another midwesterner, Elwood Haynes, demonstrated his automobile in Kokomo, Ind., in 1894, a year after the Duryeas took their horseless buggy for its first test drive on the streets of Springfield.

Haynes had not only been unaware of the Duryeas' work before he found out about it in 1895 at the Chicago race, he refused to believe that he had not been the first. In fact, for the 30 years that Haynes manufactured cars, the company's ads always carried the line: "The Haynes is America's first car."

Another of the very earliest cars makers — probably the third to go into production after Duryea and Haynes — was Alexander Winton, a short-tempered Scotsman who built his car in Cleveland.

Winton was the first to use a steering wheel instead of a tiller, he put the engine in front of the driver instead of under the car and he developed the first practical storage battery. He is also credited with signing the first franchised new-car dealer.

But he is perhaps best known now for the effect he had on others. James W. Packard, a maker of electrical products (whose firm later became the Packard Cable division of General Motors) visited Winton's office in Cleveland to offer a few suggestions for improving Winton's car. Winton blew his top and said: "If you don't like the car, why don't you build your own?" Packard did and it became one of the world's great nameplates.

On March 7, 1896, this report appeared in the Detroit Journal:

"The first horseless carriage seen in this city was out on the streets last night. The apparatus seemed to work all right and it went at the rate of five or six miles an hour at an even rate of speed."

The car was built by Charles Brady King, railroad mechanic and Chicago auto race umpire and co-driver in Mueller's Benz.

Following the car on a bicycle through the cold, snowy Detroit streets was a lanky, 32-year-old mechanical engineer who worked for the Edison Illuminating Co. His name was Henry Ford.

Roy Chapin

J.D. Maxwell

Henry Ford

Henry M. Leland

The automotive world centers in Detroit

In 1901, an oil well on a farm in Texas erupted in an incredible geyser, a steam valve blew up in New York and an auto factory burned down in Detroit.

These three seemingly unrelated events did much to make Detroit the automotive capital and to shape the still embryonic industry.

When the famous oil gusher called "Spindletop" was brought in on a farm near Beaumont, Texas, the country's petroleum production was doubled overnight. A seemingly inexhaustible supply of cheap fuel for automobiles had been discovered. The availability of low-priced fuel gave added impetus to the internal combustion engine in its competition with steam and electric power and to this day has had a tremendous impact on the U.S. car market, American attitudes toward cars and driving and the shape of the cars themselves. (You may not think it's cheap, but in constant dollars gasoline costs less today than it did 15 years ago when it was 30 cents a gallon.)

In New York, two Detroit investors, Henry B. Joy and his brother-in-law, Truman Newberry, were at the second annual New York Auto Show in 1901. Joy had decided to enter the auto business and was looking for a car company to buy.

The only car maker in Detroit was Olds and Ransom E. Olds was not interested in selling his company. Joy had been told that the Locomobile, a luxury steam car, was a likely prospect and he and Newberry were examining one when a pressure gauge exploded near Newberry's head, showering both Detroiters with hot water and dousing their interest in steamers.

They began looking for a gasoline car and were impressed with the Packard, built in Warren, Ohio, by James W. Packard. Joy bought the rights to the Packard and moved the company to Detroit. He commissioned a young architect named Albert Kahn to build a plant, which still stands on East Grand Boulevard. Kahn would design many more auto plants around the world, but from this first one would come a half-century of high-quality luxury cars.

But the Packard plant was not the first to be specially built for production of cars. The first was built in 1900 by Ransom E. Olds, a young automotive wizard from Lansing who had actually built cars and ran them several years before the Duryeas did and perhaps as early as Daimler and Benz in Germany. But they were steam-powered and Olds was coming to the view that the relatively new internal-combustion gasoline engine was the way to go.

It appears that Michigan became the center of the auto industry not because of any inexorable historical forces, or because of its geography, but because of the unique people who were there and who came to the state in those formative years.

The first Olds plant was built on East Jefferson, near the Belle Isle Bridge. While the plant was being built, Olds' engineering people designed and built 11 pilot models, including several sizes of cars and a couple of electrics.

Among them was a small, light horseless carriage with a single-cylinder, water-cooled four-cycle engine at the rear. Its most distinctive feature was its curved dashboard. The little Curved Dash Olds was a favorite in the plant, but it was not widely known to the public and was not much of a factor in the company's sales. It was considered a "mascot" or a "toy."

But in March, 1901, fire destroyed most of the Olds Motor Works and the only car that was saved was the Curved Dash Olds. Olds decided to rebuilt immediately and to put all the firm's production resources into the little Curved Dash Olds, the "Merry Oldsmobile" of musical fame.

It was a momentous decision, because it committed Olds to production of a small, relatively inexpensive car, the first "high-volume" model.

Proving the adage that it's an ill wind that blows no good, the fire had a positive effect — news of the fire made thousands of people aware of the car. Inquiries and orders began arriving, some accompanied by cash payments.

By late summer, Olds had so many orders that he sought an outside source for engines. So he went to see another man who was a potent factor in making Detroit the Motor City — Henry M. Leland, head of Leland and Faulconer Co., foremost machine shop in the Midwest. Leland agreed to build 2,000 engines for Olds. It was the first large component order by an auto maker to an outside supplier.

Olds then ordered 2,000 transmissions from a smaller machine shop owned by John and Horace Dodge. Olds announced he would produce and sell 4,000 automobiles the following year, which was equal to the total production in the United States the preceding year.

Unlike the approach used in Europe and New England of hand-building one car at a time, Olds planned to mass-produce cars, to put the world on affordable wheels. In a few years, Henry Ford would do just that, working on the foundation laid by Ransom E. Olds.

One of the ways auto makers drew attention to their vehicles in those days was to take trips in them. No one had driven from Detroit to New York, so Olds commissioned a young associate, Roy D. Chapin, to drive a Curved Dash Olds to New York for an appearance at the New York Auto Show.

(Another young associate of Olds in 1901 was John Maxwell, who later built his own car — made famous by comedian Jack Benny — and whose firm was the forerunner of Chrysler Corp.)

Chapin left Detroit on Tuesday, Oct. 29, 1901. The New York show opened the following Saturday, Nov. 2. He went through Ontario to Niagara Falls, covering 278 miles on Wednesday, an amazing performance.

He crossed into the United States on Thursday, then on Friday he encountered heavy rains between Syracuse and Albany. Wagon drivers warned him that the muddy roads were impassable.

Chapin pondered his situation. He reasoned that barges, pulled by mules, moved along the Erie Canal in any kind of weather. The towpath used by the mules was level and finished well.

On inquiring about using the towpath, he was told it was federal property and that he would be jailed if he used it. Fifteen minutes later, he pulled the little Olds onto the all-weather road that stretched along the canal to the horizon.

By evening, he was within 200 miles of his goal, the Waldorf-Astoria in New York City. Saturday he stopped to replace a bent axle, but still covered 120 miles. He planned to reach the hotel on Sunday.

But after 50 uneventful miles, his transmission developed trouble and had to be rebuilt, which took all day Monday. He started out early Tuesday and on Fifth Avenue, only blocks from the Waldorf-Astoria, he swerved to avoid hitting a man who stepped in front of the Olds. The car hit the curb and deformed a wheel. Chapin bent it back as best he could and drove on.

Roy Chapin, who would later head the Hudson Motor Car Co. and whose son, Roy Jr., would head American Motors Corp., had completed the longest automobile trip that had been made in this country up until that time. Ransom Olds was waiting in the lobby of the hotel to greet him, but Chapin — covered with grease and dust — was ordered by the doorman to use the service entrance at the rear of the hotel.

Of all the automotive giants of that era, undoubtedly the most underestimated has been Henry Leland. It is virtually impossible to overstate his contributions to the auto industry. Yet his hame never appeared on a car's nameplate and the only remembrances of him in the Motor City he did so much to create are names on a street and a former hotel.

This man built engines for Olds, the first mass-produced car in the world and the first to be produced in Detroit. He improved the Olds engine by redesigning valve ports and raising its compression and offered it to Olds, who turned him down.

So in 1902, Leland took the engine to a meeting of directors of the Henry Ford Co., who had gathered to close the business. The company had been formed by four investors to exploit the work of Ford, but there had been a misunderstanding and Ford had quit the company, so it had nothing to build or sell.

(Disagreements between the strong-willed inventors who designed and built cars and the hard-headed businessmen who backed them financially were not unusual. Olds also disagreed with his financial backers and left the company, which kept the name Oldsmobile. He went back to Lansing whence he came and built a car bearing his initials, the Reo. The original Oldsmobile company, which became a division of General Motors, also moved to Lansing.)

Leland's engine was so compact that he could carry it into the room. The directors were impressed and after Leland's presentation, decided to build a car using this advanced motor.

But the car was not called the Leland. At Leland's suggestion, it was named after the French explorer who founded Detroit, Antoine de la Mothe Cadillac. With its small, efficient single-cylinder engine, the "one-lunger" Cadillac was an immediate success.

As the master machinist, Leland achieved a degree of interchangeability of parts that had been sought but not quite reached by Olds. After rigorous testing by the Royal Automobile Club in Great Britain, the Cadillac was the first American car to win the club's Dewar Trophy for distinguished automotive achievement.

Leland would later sell his Cadillac company to General Motors and serve as an executive running that division, then leave the corporation after disagreements over just how high the quality of the car should be and a heated dispute over the corporation's role in World War I.

He started another company to build aircraft engines for the war effort, later shifted to automobile production. He named his new car after a longtime hero of his and the Lincoln became a competitor to Cadillac and Packard in the luxury-car market. (Leland later sold Lincoln to Ford Motor Co.)

Leland's influence was also personal. On one occasion, Leland lectured the head of a leading supplier of roller bearings on the importance of precision machining. Leland had measured some bearings with a micrometer and said to him:

"Your Mr. Steenstrup told me these bearings would be accurate to 1,000th of an inch. But look here (pointing out variations). Even though you make thousands, the first and last should be precisely alike."

On the receiving end of the lecture was Alfred P. Sloan Jr., head of Hyatt Roller Bearing Co., later to become the legendary head of General Motors and architect of modern American management theory.

Of his encounter with Leland, Sloan said many years later: "A genuine conception of what mass production should mean really grew in me with that conversation."

Henry Ford and the Model T

William Durant and the first Chevrolet

David D. Buick and his first car

A homespun genius and an empire builder

The residents along Bagley Ave. between Grand River and Clifford may have been startled by the commotion in the middle of a June night in 1896, but they soon figured out it must be Henry Ford and that contraption of his. It was.

About 2 a.m., Henry's wife, Clara, was probably not too surprised to see that the strange and brilliant man she had married was battering down a brick wall in the shed in which he had been building his "quadricycle," the name he gave his horseless carriage.

It was perhaps typical of Ford's genius that he had figured out how to build this complex machine, but had not planned how he would get it out of the shed when it was finished.

So he broke down the wall with an ax, pushed the quadricycle out onto Bagley and spun the fly-wheel. It coughed into action as Ford drove it down the street in a test run that would change the world forever.

Ford was not the first to build a car that worked, not even the first in Detroit. Three months earlier, Charles B. King had driven the first car on the streets of the city. In Chicago, Frank and Charles Duryea had raced their car and had begun producing it in Massachusetts. Ransom E. Olds, Elwood Haynes and Alexander Winton had all built automobiles in the United States and in Europe a number of cars were already in production.

But Ford envisioned building cars for everyone, not just the rich. He did not intend to build them one at a time, he wanted to mass-produce them from inter-changeable parts.

William Durant, unlike most of the early automotive pioneers, was not a tinkerer or a mechanic or an inventor — he was a salesman. In fact, he was a superb salesman; he could, in the words of one associate, "charm the birds from the trees."

Grandson of a Michigan governor and a self-made milliionaire in the horse-drawn carriage manufacturing business, Durant did not like the new automobiles that were beginning to appear around his home town of Flint. They were noisy and smelly, he said, and they frightened the animals.

His feeling that the new machines were obnoxious was not a reaction against something that might threaten his Durant-Dort Carriage Co., largest maker of horse-drawn carriages in the country. He was a success, no doubt about it, a millionaire several times over. He did not fear innovation, he thrived on it. In fact, he drove a steam-powered Mobile car in 1902, not because he might want to buy one, but because he might want to sell them. He was unimpressed with it and with automobiles generally. Until, that is, he drove a car in 1904 built by David Dunbar Buick.

Buick was an innovative fellow who had made a fortune in the plumbing business, largely because he figured out how to porcelainize cast iron for tubs and sinks. He began to manufacture gasoline engines in 1900 and decided to design an automobile. But his business foundered. He tinkered a lot, but he did not produce cars commercially.

In 1903, Benjamin and Frank Briscoe rook over Buick's business, then sold it to J.H. Whiting, owner of the Flint Wagon Works. Whiting convinced Durant to drive the Buick car, which featured a valve-in-head engine. Durant was impressed.

In 1904, Durant reorganized Buick Motor Co. and embarked on a remarkable adventure of empire building in which he created General Motors, lost it, created Chevrolet and took GM back. He finally lost it again, but he had a good time and he never lost heart.

After a couple of false starts (including the Henry Ford Co., which later became Cadillac), Ford founded the present Ford Motor Co. in 1903 backed by 12 investors, including Detroit coal dealer Alexander Malcolmson, his bookkeeper James Couzens and John and Horace Dodge, who had built transmissions for Olds and were now to supply engines to Ford.

It did not take long for Ford's chronically stormy relationship with investors to begin. Irked by Malcolmson's investment in another auto company, he formed a subsidiary, Ford Manufacturing Co., in 1905 to produce engines and other components, but mainly to cut Malcolmson out. Malcolmson owned no interest in the new subsidiary, the entity which paid dividends.

In rapid succession, Ford sold his first car on July 23, 1903, set a world record by driving his Old 999 racing car at 91 miles per hour on frozen Lake St. Clair in 1904, went international with formation of Ford Motor Co. of Canada in 1904, acquired over half of Ford Motor Co. stock in 1906 and, on Oct. 1, 1908, introduced the Model T. The automotive revolution was under way.

The car was priced at $850 and it was Ford's notion of a "universal" car — small, light, inexpensive and reliable. The Ford Model T, the beloved "Tin Lizzie," made Henry Ford the world's leading industrialist and folk hero.

The Model T was produced with only minor changes for 19 years. When production ended in 1927, more than 15 million were built. In some years, the Model T accounted for more than half of the cars sold in the United States. To meet the enormous demand for the car, Ford built the River Rouge complex. He plowed so much money into the venture that the Dodge brothers led a stockholders' revolt and finally sold out to Ford for $25 million. Ford bought out all the stockholders for an estimated $100 million and the company was entirely family-owned for 35 years.

Ford was not content to write automotive history with his product alone. He refused to pay royalties to holders of the Selden patent. George B. Selden, a Rochester, N.Y., attorney and inventor who had never built a car, applied for and received a patent for the automobile in 1895. Most auto makers produced cars under a license and paid royalties to holders of the patent. Ford refused.

After a long legal battle, the U.S. Court of Appeals ruled in 1911 that the four-cycle engines Ford was building were not covered by the patent. Since most builders were making four-cycle engines, the patent was broken and Henry Ford's status of folk hero was enhanced.

In 1914, he announced the $5 day for workers at his company and thereby enraged fellow industrialists, but the people loved him. He expounded a consumerist economic theory — if more cars are to be sold, people must be able to afford them.

He kept cutting the price of the Model T until it reached $265 for a roadster in mid-1923. Some people thought he was crazy, but most thought he was a humanitarian and a genius.

In 1914, he sent rebate checks to buyers of Model Ts, an unprecedented act. That same year, a group of pacifists talked him into financing a "Peace Ship," which would seek to halt the war in Europe. This peace enterprise, as so many do, split up in quarrels and Ford went into his stateroom and refused to talk to anyone.

But his prestige was such that his naivete was forgiven and he was widely praised.

After achieving success with the Buick car, Durant formed General Motors in New Jersey in 1908 and it bought Buick. With breathtaking speed, Durant's new GM acquired Oldsmobile, Cadillac and Oakland (later to be Pontiac), plus some supplier firms and a few lesser auto makers. In its first year of existence, GM had put together all of its current car-producing divisions except Chevrolet.

In its first two years, Durant had brought 30 firms into GM, including 11 auto makers. Not all of Durant's ventures were successful, however. He bought the Heany Electric Co., which was based on John Albert Heany's patent for an electric light bulb. General Electric sued and before the case was over, Heany, his lawyer and a patent office clerk were indicted on charges of falsifying the application. Heany was later exonerated, but the others went to jail and Durant lost faith in the inventor.

GM lost a lot of money in the Heany affair and it was undoubtedly a factor in the corporation's weakened financial condition which led to the ousting of Durant. A group of Eastern bankers agreed to bail out GM. They favored dissolving the company, but Wilfred Leland talked them out of it.

Instead, the bankers were to receive an enormous bloc of stock and control of the board of directors. Durant was to resign and a five-man committee would run GM for the duration of the loan. Durant had lost his empire.

Durant did not retire from action, however. He formed a number of companies, including Chevrolet Motor Co. in partnership with Louis Chevrolet. Durant met Louis and Arthur Chevrolet when they came to America as part of a French racing team. (Louis was the more aggressive and more successful race driver of the two, so the prudent Durant hired Arthur as his chauffeur.)

Louis Chevrolet had built a

high-quality car with his name on it. While Chevrolet was visiting Europe in 1913, Durant changed the design to a smaller car in an attempt to achieve high volume. The Royal Mail and the Baby Grand were the first to sport the now-famous Chevrolet "bowtie" insignia. Chevrolet didn't like what Durant had done. He quit the company.

Meanwhile, Durant's Chevrolets were a great sales success. The company grew rapidly and Durant used profits to buy up GM stock. GM, meanwhile, was coming back out of trouble under the guidance of Charles Nash, a Durant protege who was president of GM, and the new head of Buick, Walter P. Chrysler.

By the time of the board meeting in 1916, Durant's Chevrolet had bought up almost half of the outstanding GM stock. Nash, unaware of that, called Durant aside before the meeting. The trust agreement was running out and the majority of the board had agreed to renew it, Nash told Durant. "So let's not have any trouble."

"There won't be any trouble, Charlie," Durant said. "We won't renew the agreement, but there won't be any trouble. It just so happens that I own General Motors."

Durant nominated Pierre du Pont, who was trusted by the bankers, as chairman. Chevrolet was to be merged into GM. By the following May, the deal was complete and Durant had GM again. He met with Nash.

"Well, Charlie, you're through," he told his former employe who he felt had thrown in his lot with the bankers.

Durant became president of GM for the first time. He would lose it again, but in early 1917, GM was strong and the future looked bright.

Walter P. Chrysler and the first Chrysler

Chevrolet assembly line, 1916

1927 Chevrolet

Chrysler leaves GM and makes it the Big Three

Among the many auto companies which William Durant bought for General Motors in its first few years was one owned by Byron T. Carter, who designed the friction-drive Cartercar.

In December, 1910, Carter stopped to help a woman whose car had stalled on Detroit's Belle Isle Bridge. As Carter hand-cranked her engine, it backfired, spinning the crank backward. The crank broke Carter's arm and shattered his jaw. Two Cadillac engineers passing by on the way to work took Carter to a hospital, where he developed pneumonia and died.

Cranking engines by hand was the way to start them in those early years and it was a hazardous undertaking. It took considerable strength and broken arms and other injuries were not uncommon.

Henry Leland, head of GM's Cadillac Division, knew Carter and was horrified when he heard of his death. He assigned a group of Cadillac engineers to find a solution. They did: Charles F. Kettering.

While an engineer at National Cash Register Co. in Dayton, Ohio, Kettering had invented a small, high-torque electric motor to replace the hand crank on cash registers. Kettering and Edward Deeds, who had been sales manager at NCR, set up their own company, Dayton Engineering Laboratories Co. (Delco) to make and market an auto ignition system Kettering had designed. One customer was Cadillac.

Two months after Kettering and his associate, William A. Chryst, began work on the auto starter, they gave a demonstration of it and Cadillac bought it. In fact,

Cadillac bought more than a starter, because Kettering had integrated the starter -- adapted from the cash register motor -- into a complete ignition and electrical system which included a battery recharged by a generator run by the engine and electric headlights to replace acetylene lamps.

The system was installed on Cadillac's 1912 model, one of those very few cars that was truly an automotive milestone.

Kettering's system -- basically still used by every maker in the world -- opened motoring to a vastly greater public.

Upon regaining control of General Motors in 1916, William Durant's first act was to fire Charles W. Nash, who was president of GM during its period of control by the Eastern bankers. Nash took over the ailing Jeffery Motors (which became Nash, then Nash-Kelvinator and in 1954 merged with Hudson to form American Motors). His second was to give Walter P. Chrysler a raise.

Chrysler was head of Buick, a job for which Nash, no spendthrift, had paid him $50,000 a year. Durant had heard that Chrysler was making a bid to take over Packard and he offered him $500,000 a year to continue at Buick. Chrysler stayed.

That same year, Durant made one of GM's most important acquisitions: United Motors Corp., a combination of parts and accessories makers which included Delco, New Departure and Hyatt Roller Bearing Co. In addition to the products it brought into the GM fold, it also brought in Delco's Kettering and the president of Hyatt, Alfred P. Sloan Jr.

Part of the deal when Durant regained GM was a division of the board of directors -- six named by Durant, six by the bankers and three to be neutral. Pierre S. du Pont, head of the chemical giant, became chairman, nominated by Durant and trusted by all. One of the neutrals was John Jacob Raskob, a close du Pont aide. In the years ahead, Johnny Raskob turned out to be Durant's most powerful ally in his empire-building spree.

When the United States entered World War I, Henry Leland, along with his son and close associate at Cadillac, Wilfred, told Durant they wanted to convert a new Cadillac body plant to production of airplane engines to help the war effort. The Lelands were anglophiles, Durant was not. He told them no GM facility would produce war materiel.

The Lelands wrestled with their feelings for weeks, then on July 3, 1917, they quit GM. Six weeks later, they organized Lincoln Motor Co. to build airplane engines. In 1920, they built the first Lincoln car to challenge Cadillac in the luxury-car field.

With the end of the war came boom times for the auto business. Durant began buying companies, including a 60 percent interest in Fisher Body. In 1919, GM of Canada and General Motors Acceptance Corp. were created. Encouraged by Raskob, who was able to secure financing with du Pont money and connections, Durant continued to expand GM's empire, ignoring more cautious voices.

Durant ordered construction of the General Motors Building on West Grand Blvd. in Detroit, to be the largest office building in the world. (In fact, it was to be called the Durant Building and it has the initial "D" at its corners near the top in the manner of Napoleon, who decreed the letter "N" be put on buildings erected in Paris during his reign.)

Then in 1920, the bubble burst.

Irked by Durant's management style, Chrysler quit. The action shook GM, particularly Sloan.

Car sales declined, inventories began mounting, the bond market weakening and GM was in a financial bind. GM's stock price slid, despite heavy buying by Durant with his personal fortune in an effort to prop up the stock. He bought on margin, often only 10 percent.

Fearful that his personal failure would be tied to GM, which itself owed $80 million to the banks, the bankers demanded that Durant resign. Raskob and du Pont came up with a proposal to buy Durant out. Forced to sell at $9.50, he had lost about $100 million of his own money.

The deal was consummated and he resigned on a Friday. Monday, GM opened at $16.50. What Durant had failed to do with his millions of dollars, he finally did by resigning. GM was turned around.

Durant had wanted nothing in the world so much as to run GM, but that was not the case with the man who succeeded him. Pierre S. du Pont was only 50, but had retired from running the family chemical firm because he had more important projects in mind: cultivating plants at his greenhouse on Longwood, his estate near Wilmington, Del., and pushing educational reforms in the Delaware schools.

He had become chairman of GM in 1915 to help the company he and his friends had invested in, but Durant had run the company. But by the time Durant resigned in 1920, the DuPont Co. owned 43 percent of GM and du Pont could not just walk away.

While president and chairman, du Pont managed to get involved in one of Kettering's few ideas which didn't work out, an air-cooled engine with copper fins to pass off heat. Du Pont thought it would be just the thing to power a low-priced car to compete with Ford's Model T. Sloan was cool to the idea, because there were serious manufacturing problems.

In a curious way, Henry Ford set in motion a chain of events that would lead to Chevrolet's ill-fated production of the copper-cooled engine and the elevation of Sloan to the presidency of General Motors.

Signius Wilhelm Poul Knudsen was a big, beefy Dane who arrived in the United States at age 20. He took a job at the John R. Keim Mills in Buffalo, where a timekeeper decided he was "William S. Knudsen," because he was not going to fool around with any name like "Signius."

Knudsen developed a method for forming and drawing steel and Keim Mills became a major supplier of pressed steel parts. Ford bought the company and gave Knudsen a raise. Knudsen got married, one of his better moves, because his wife, Clara Euler, proved to be a civilizing influence on the hard-driving, hot-tempered, blaspheming Knudsen.

Knudsen organized 14 Model T assembly plants in two years and then three more in Europe, including one in his native Denmark. He became one of Ford's top executives and, like so many since, this led directly to his departure from the company.

Ford did not like to surround himself with strong men, or with men who smoked, drank and swore. Knudsen was guilty on all counts. In February, 1921, stung by public rebukes from Ford, Knudsen quit.

Ten months later, he was hired by Charles S. Mott, vice president of GM's accessories division, for $6,000 a year (he had been making $50,000 a year at Ford). A month later, Sloan made him Chevrolet production vice president at $30,000 a year.

When Knudsen, a can-do kind of guy, said he could produce 500 copper-cooled Chevrolets a month, the scale was tipped to du Pont. The copper-cooled Chevrolet went into production and 250 were built in time for the New York Auto Show in January, 1923.

Knudsen admitted production

problems were greater than anticipated, but Kettering's engine required less maintenance, weighed less and got better mileage than conventional water-cooled engines.

The cars had not been in the hands of the public long before complaints started. The engine overheated, causing all sorts of problems. Kettering's design was not as efficient as other air-cooled units, such as the Franklin's.

The decisive Knudsen recalled all the copper-cooled cars and had many of them dumped into Lake Erie.

Du Pont brooded about the episode and his role in it. That he had made an error in judgment was not so bad. That he had become emotionally involved to the extent that his judgment was impeded was, he felt, inexcusable.

Du Pont resigned as president and recommended that Sloan succeed him.

In 1923, the Sloan era began at GM, an era that would transform the corporation, the American auto industry and American industry in general.

After Chrysler resigned from GM in 1920, he agreed to manage the financially troubled Willys-Overland. While there, he put together an engineering team under Fred Zeder, who had been with Studebaker, which developed an advanced, high-compression engine.

As Willys-Overland returned to financial health, the bankers who had drafted Chrysler for the job asked him to do the same for Maxwell, a Detroit auto maker which was in serious difficulty. Chrysler bought the Willys engine plant and Zeder's engine for Maxwell and began building a new car at the old Chalmers plant in Detroit.

Several models of this Maxwell, which had the name "Chrysler" on it, were shipped to New York for the 1924 auto show. But because the car had never been sold as a production model, it was not eligible for exhibition.

This was bad news, because Chrysler was not only looking for sales orders, he needed financing. He showed the cars in the lobby of the Hotel Commodore and manned the exhibit himself, selling a number of cars and securing from Ed Tinker, president of Chase Securities, the financing he needed.

"It was the only way I could get away from him," Tinker later joked of his wise investment in the supersalesman and his car.

Later that year, Maxwell-Chalmers was reorganized into Chrysler Corp. Detroit had its Big Three.

Edsel and Henry Ford inspect experimental V-8 for 1932

Above: Alfred P. Sloan Jr.
Left: William Knudsen
1927 Cadillac LaSalle designed by Harley J. Earl

Mr. Sloan, Harley Earl and dynamic obsolescence

"Dependability" is a common enough word today, but it did not begin appearing in dictionaries until the early '30s. It was a word coined by the men who sold the cars that John and Horace Dodge began building in late 1914.

Letters from buyers of those early Dodges praised the car's power and rugged construction, but their most consistent comment was that the car could be depended upon. It did not take Dodge marketing people long to begin talking about the car's "dependability." (The word was coined by Theodore MacManus, who also wrote the famous "penalty of leadership" ad for Cadillac.)

The Dodge brothers were legendary figures in the early auto industry. Born in poverty in Niles, Mich., they amassed enormous fortunes building transmissions for the Curved Dash Olds and engines for Ford Motor Co.

They were stockholders of Ford Motor Co. and John was a vice president of Ford. They would regularly offer improvements to Ford cars -- until the Model T. The Model T was Ford's baby and he would brook no tampering with it.

In November, 1914, the Dodge brothers began building their own car, which incorporated many improvements they had offered Ford.

John and Horace Dodge were famous for their saloon escapades, drinking and roughhousing. The public announcement that the Dodges would build their own motor car was made at a party in Detroit's fashionable Book-Cadillac Hotel, capped by John Dodge marching up and down the banquet tables, darkening the hall by smashing light bulbs in the chandeliers with a cane.

But "dependability" described the Dodge brothers in their business dealings as well as their cars and they were just as well known for their integrity as for their escapades.

Gen. John Pershing used Dodge cars to chase Pancho Villa and other Mexican bandits back over the border. American troops used three Dodge touring cars to charge bandit headquarters 200 miles south of El Paso, destroying the rebellion without American casualties and making history as the first motorized combat operation by the U.S. Army.

The Dodges played another important role in military technology when French Marshal Joseph Joffre visited Washington in search of an American firm that could make the delicate recoil firing mechanisms for French 75 and 155 cannons, which were the backbone of the Allied artillery effort in World War I. Secretary of War Newton D. Baker called on John Dodge.

Dodge told Joffre and Baker that if the French provided his firm with accurate blueprints and left the project entirely to Dodge management, the mechanism could be produced in any quantity desired. Joffre and Baker did not think it was possible to mass-pro-duce the mechanism and so informed Dodge.

"The hell is isn't," Dodge said.

"I am not accustomed to being spoken to in that kind of language," said Baker.

"The war would be a hell of a lot better off if you were," Dodge shouted back. "Do you want us to do this job or don't you?"

The Dodges did the job and after the war the French Government awarded the Legion of Honor to John Dodge and his 8,000 workmen.

The Dodge brothers had their differences and quarrels, but through most of their lives they were inseparable and they were in death also. They died within a year of each other in 1920.

Their widows asked Frederick Haynes, manager of the Dodge plant in Hamtramck, to run the company. Under Haynes, the company continued to grow and acquired Graham Truck in 1925, which became Dodge Truck. Joseph, Robert and Ray Graham worked for Dodge for a while, then left to build the Graham-Paige car.

In 1925, the widows of John and Horace Dodge sold Dodge Brothers Motor Car Co. to the New York banking syndicate of Dillon, Read and Co. for $146 million, biggest cash deal up to that time in the auto industry. Less than three years later, the bankers sold it to Chrysler Corp. for $170 million.

Pierre du Pont resigned as president of General Motors in 1923, in part at least, as a result of the copper-cooled engine affair. And the first crisis Alfred P. Sloan Jr. faced as president was also a result of that debacle. Research wizard Charles Kettering, discouraged by the failure and rejection of his engine, resigned.

Sloan knew that du Pont, still chairman of the board, would be upset by Kettering's departure. He also knew that Kettering was a genius and Sloan did not want to lose him. So Sloan proposed to Kettering that he head a new GM Research Corp. to be established in Dayton. Kettering would be paid $120,000 a year, $20,000 more than Sloan was being paid.

Kettering accepted the offer. The copper-cooled engine issue faded quickly. The hard feelings cooled and soon they were "Alfred" and "Ket" again. (Kettering and Chrysler were the only colleagues to call Sloan by his first name; to everyone else, he was "Mr. Sloan.")

The research operation paid for itself many times over through the years. And Sloan turned to a more

enjoyable and absorbing task: taking advantage of the auto sales boom just getting under way and making sure that GM made a profit, good times or bad.

Sloan had organized GM management along the lines of the German Army under Bismarck, using a staff-line concept. With only minor changes, that organization served GM for 50 years. Business administration students studied it and most major American corporations adopted some form of it.

After losing $38.6 million in 1921, the first annual loss sustained by the corporation, two financial whizzes brought in by du Pont — Donaldson Brown and Albert Bradley — developed plans to assure that it would not happen again.

Du Pont had brought Brown from the chemical company to GM, where he served as treasurer and later vice president in charge of finance. Brown was a gifted executive, although his financial jargon, pedantic lectures and charts and graphs did not endear him to his colleagues, one of whom is said to have complained that Brown "didn't speak any known language."

Brown worked out the "standard volume" concept, a financial strategy that has endured with little change to the present. GM would set its prices to produce a 20 percent return on investment based on what it sells in an average year. When sales were above average, profits soared. When they slumped, the company would still make a profit.

The theory got a quick test. In 1924, the anticipated spring upsurge in sales did not materialize. Dealers had heavy inventories of cars. Sloan ordered divisions to cut production and lay off workers.

The result was that the workers bore much of the hardship of the downturn. This would become the general pattern: when times were bad, dealers and workers bore most of the brunt. Donaldson Brown's concept worked. GM sales in 1924 were way off from the preceding year, but GM earned a 20 percent return on investment.

All through the Great Depression of the '30s, GM never had a losing year. In fact, it would never lose money again until 1980.

The recession of 1924 put severe financial pressure on Oakland Motor Car Co., which had never been one of GM's stronger divisions. Sloan ordered design of a car using as many Chevrolet parts as possible and priced between Chevrolet and Oldsmobile. Charles Mott suggested the name for the new car: Pontiac.

GM had been running well behind Ford in sales, but had been slowly closing the gap. In 1924, GM accounted for about 19 percent of U.S. new-car sales, Ford for just over 50 percent. The next year, GM cut Ford's lead to 42-20, then the next year to 35-28.

When Chevrolet introduced a new model in 1925, it was competing with a Ford Model T so old in its design and so different from its contemporaries that some states required a special license to drive it. The handwriting was on the wall. The days of the Model T, the most successful car in history, were numbered.

If any year had to be picked as the dividing line between the old auto industry and the modern, 1924 is a likely candidate. When Sloan ordered design of the car that became the Pontiac, it was the first to be fitted to a particular market slot and the first to use parts from a sister car.

He also wanted cars that would offer new features to bring in customers and convince them to change cars. Almost everyone owned a car by 1925. Now cars would have to be sold almost entirely to current car owners.

This last factor, which developed into what was benignly called annual model changes and which critics termed "planned obsolescence," was perhaps the most far-reaching in its implications for the auto industry

In addition to ordering the car that became the 1926 Pontiac, Sloan also assigned Cadillac to come up with a family car to fill the gap between Buick and Cadillac. The LaSalle, introduced in 1927, was another of those rare landmark cars that change the industry forever. But its innovation was not technological, as was the 1912 Cadillac's; it was designed not by engineers and body builders, but by a new automotive breed, a stylist.

Lawrence Fisher, one of the brothers of Fisher Body fame who became head of Cadillac Division, had noticed that the best-looking Cadillacs at the New York Auto Show had bodies designed by Harley J. Earl, a Hollywood customizer of cars for the stars.

Fisher hired Earl to act as consultant on the LaSalle, which was to be lower-priced and less conservative than the Cadillac. The Hollywood designer, who sometimes appeared in the staid Detroit automotive studios in jodhpurs and riding boots, seemed eccentric to GM brass, but they liked his work.

After the '27 LaSalle, Earl designed the '28 Cadillac, then went back to Hollywood. But not for long. Sloan made him an offer he couldn't refuse: a newly formed Art and Color Section, which he would head, to style all of GM's car lines.

In 1927, Ford Motor Co. halted production of the Model T after more than 15 million had been built. It was truly the car that had put the United States on wheels, but it was out of date.

Henry's son, Edsel, was now president of Ford Motor Co. and had been pushing to expand Ford's offerings to meet the GM challenge and wanted more elegant styling. But the Model A was still Henry's. Edsel would get his elegant styling later, in the '30s. Ford was out of production for much of 1927 while the Model A was being readied and GM beat it in sales for the first time.

The Model A was an overnight sensation and Ford recovered the lead in 1928. Henry did not like the new approach GM was taking to styling and annual model changes, but the die was cast. It quickly became apparent the Model A would not be built for 19 years as the Model T had been. GM passed Ford in sales in 1931 and Ford never regained the lead.

In 1932, Ford tried to stem the challenge of established GM and upstart Chrysler by introducing the first low-priced car powered by a V-8 engine. Ford sales improved, but GM was still No. 1.

In 1933, Chrysler Corp. also passed Ford in sales. The sales race was on.

'Looney gas' survives and changes engine

After revolutionizing the auto industry with his electric self-starter, Kettering turned to another problem just beginning to cause worry. Cadillac engineers complained that Kettering's self-starter and battery ignition system was making spark plugs misfire, causing knocking in the cylinders.

But Kettering didn't think the plugs were misfiring. He suspected it was a problem with the fuel. As engines were designed to compress the fuel/air charge to a greater extent, engines were able to extract more power from the fuel. But the greater the compression, the greater the knock, Kettering found. The higher compression was causing the fuel to ignite before the spark. This pre-ignition was causing the knock.

The more efficient high-compression engines were necessary not only to make cars run faster, but because experts had determined in 1915 that the world's oil supply would be depleted by 1940.

Kettering assigned an assistant, Thomas Midgley Jr., to search for a compound to make the fuel less volatile, less likely to pre-ignite under compression, while retaining its high density of energy. Even though new discoveries of oil in Texas made it clear that the predictions of running out of oil were greatly exaggerated, Kettering and Midgley contin-

ued the search because higher-compression engines ran better and more smoothly, provided much more power and delivered greater fuel economy.

A number of chemical compounds were tried, including tellurium, which showed great promise for halting premature ignition, but smelled strongly of garlic. Its smell was so strong and it so completely defied all efforts to banish it that the researchers gave up and searched for something else.

In 1922, Midgley announced he had found it — tetraethyl lead. It would eliminate premature ignition, he said, and could increase gasoline mileage by 25 percent.

The first ethyl gasoline went on sale in Dayton in early 1923. It was called "premium" gasoline.

GM formed the General Motors Chemical Co., with Kettering as chairman and Midgley as president. It contracted to buy tetraethyl compound from DuPont.

GM then approached Standard Oil of New Jersey and the two companies formed Ethyl Gasoline Corp., which proved to be a very profitable venture. Until it all blew up in October, 1924.

An explosion in Standard Oil's research lab in Baywater, N.J., left 35 men seriously ill from inhaling fumes of tetraethyl lead. Eight were hospitalized and five of them died, one of them in a straightjacket because he had gone quite mad.

Newspapers headlined the effects of "looney gas" and a nationwide panic was started. New Jersey suspended sales of the compound and sales across the country collapsed.

Rumors circulated about poor devils who had gone crazy while motoring. This extremely important advance in automotive technology was in grave peril. In addition to being technologically important, it was extremely lucrative.

GM and Standard hesitated, hoping to ride out the storm of damaging publicity. Six more men died at DuPont's tetraethyl plant. GM and Standard ordered sales halted.

Scientists at Du Pont were well aware of the dangers in manufacturing tetraethyl lead, but they also knew it was perfectly safe in the greatly diluted form in which it appeared in gasoline (less than 1/10th of one percent by volume).

A federal committee appointed to investigate came to the same conclusion. Du Pont was willing to handle the risks and there was no danger to the public. A little over a year later, after an intensive advertising campaign, premium gasoline was back on the market.

Aiding in acceptance of ethyl was the popularity of the cars built by Walter Chrysler's new company, cars with high-compression engines.

One problem that GM had in its battle with Ford in the early '20s was that it was up against a myth, a legend, a national folk hero. Henry Ford himself was one of the most famous men in history.

His attitude toward workers was suspect in many ways, but his $5 day had made him legendary. His peace ship venture had ended in failure and bickering, but his attempt had made him a hero. He had beaten the "vested interests" in breaking the Selden patent. And the Model T held an almost sacred position in the American mind.

But GM found a way to fight this: installment credit, a concept which was anathema to Henry Ford.

The automobile had quickly become not only a necessity to Americans, but also a status symbol. Pushed on by "easy-payment" credit, ownership of a car had become a symbol of success.

Installment buying spread to many product lines and was a driving force of the prosperity of the '20s.

Used-car dealers used easy-credit plans to clear their lots and to cut into sales of Ford's Model T, the greatest entry-level car ever built in America. The price of the Model T had dropped to as low as $265 in the mid-'20s. Ford's solution for all his woes to cut prices. But he refused to offer a time-payment plan and thereby contributed to his beloved Model T's decline.

But Ford's opposition to credit buying did not stop his greatest constituency, the farmers, from mortgaging their land to buy Model Ts and Fordson tractors.

The auto industry had given the American farmer the means to an agricultural revolution from which everyone benefited but the farmer.

With modern farm machinery, farmers were able to increase their yields, thus driving down the price of their crops. At the same time, their own costs increased, because the new technology was not cheap. This paradoxical problem of increased efficiency undermining the prosperity of the farmer persists to this day.

The American farmer, aided by tractors, modern farm implements and new fertilizers and pesticides, became the wonder of the world. And low crop prices drove more of them off the farm and into the cities. The Great Depression started with the stock market crash in October, 1929. But a rural depression preceded it by several years.

By 1925, almost three-quarters of all automobiles sold were sold on credit. Still true in the 101st year of the automobile.

Clockwise from right: '37 Volkswagen;
'37 Packard; '37 Cord; '34 Chrysler
Airflow; '37 Ford V-8

Hard times slim industry, Detroit starts selling dreams

A famous car of the '20s was the Jordan Playboy. Despite its flashy name, it was a mediocre car. Sales never hit 10,000 a year and it was gone before the stock market crashed in 1929.

It is remembered because of an ad that its maker, Ned Jordan, wrote in 1923. The ad, headed "Somewhere West of Laramie," did not dwell on the technical aspects of the Playboy. In fact, it did not mention them.

"Somewhere west of Laramie there's a bronco-busting, steer-roping girl who knows what I'm talking about," Jordan wrote (so legend has it) on an envelope while riding a train over the Wyoming plains bound for San Francisco. "She can tell what a sassy pony that's a cross between greased lightning and the place where it hits, can do with eleven hundred pounds of steel and action when he's going high, wide and handsome.

"The truth is — the Playboy was built for her."

The ad, which was published just a week after Jordan feverishly penned it and forever changed the marketing of cars, went on in this vein, then concluded:

"Step into the Playboy when the hour grows dull with things grown dead and stale. Then start for the land of real living with the spirit of the lass who rides, lean and rangy, into the red horizon of a Wyoming twilight."

In the '20s, just about every family had a car. The automobile was accepted and reliable. There were literally hundreds of nameplates to choose from and now cars had to be sold to buyers who by and large already owned one. And they all functioned in more or less the same way.

So what made a Jordan Playboy different? Romance. Or, as we call it today, image. Apparently not too many customers bought it. But the industry did.

Detroit began selling not only cars but dreams.

In 1929, the year the stock market crash in October triggered the Great Depression, new-car sales in the United States totaled a then-record 3,848,937. They would not reach that level again for 20 years.

The crash hit the auto industry with incredible impact. In September, General Motors stock sold for $73. It fell by half in October. In 1932, it bottomed out at $8.

In 1929, U.S. auto plants produced more than 5.5 million cars and trucks. By 1932, output fell to less than 1.4 million.

Many nameplates fell by the wayside during the Depression. Essex gave up in 1931, Franklin (of air-cooled fame) in 1934, Reo (Ransom E. Olds' second automotive venture) in 1936 and the magnificent Pierce-Arrow went under in 1937.

The Auburn Automobile Co., Auburn Ind., produced three American classics, the Auburn, the Cord and the Duesenberg, all of which went out of production during the Depression.

The Duesenberg was arguably the finest car ever built in this country, America's answer to the Rolls-Royce and the Bugatti. Styled in-house by Gordon Buehrig or with custom body by the most prestigious coachmakers, the Duesenberg J was the ultimate automobile and the ultimate status symbol.

The final nail in the Auburn company's coffin was driven by one of its most magnificent products, the Cord 810, introduced in 1936, and the upscale 812, introduced in 1937. Also designed by Buehrig, the front-wheel-drive car was powered by a V-8 engine and had a body so advanced that it still looks modern, with retractable headlights, wraparound grille, and chromed exhaust headers.

The car created a sensation, but the company had trouble getting it built, ran out of money and collapsed.

When Auburn folded, dies for the Buehrig Cord were adapted by Graham for its 1940 Hollywood model and by Hupmobile for its '41 Skylark. It was the last gasp for both these nameplates, although Graham-Paige Co. survived as part of the basis for Kaiser-Frazer after World War II (Joseph W. Frazer was president of Graham-Paige).

The "Big Three" survived the Depression, in fact GM made

money and Chrysler actually grew. Ford Motor Co. was wounded almost mortally, although nobody knew it because it was not a public company and its bookkeeping was bizarrely primitive.

The Oakland and LaSalle nameplates were dropped by GM and Chrysler brought out its very modern Airflow in 1935, which did not sell well, but which established a number of design principles — unibody construction, engine forward of the front axle and all seats within the axles, among others — which quickly spread through the industry.

Among the stronger independents, Nash dropped its Lafayette and Hudson sales declined, but its Terraplane carried it. Packard continued to lead the luxury-car segment, but the annual model change and changing demographics were already weakening its position. Packard was the car of the old moneyed class, while Cadillac was favored by the emerging new rich. The Depression was eroding the old aristocracy and when prosperity returned after World War II, Cadillac soared and Packard was doomed.

Studebaker brought out its low-priced Rockne (named for the popular Notre Dame football coach) in time to get chewed up by Ford's Model A and it bought into Pierce-Arrow just as the luxury-car market was collapsing, but it survived a financial crisis in 1933 and came back to play an important role in the post-war boom market of the '40s.

As the auto market became more competitive, the push for mechanical progress became intense and the Depression was a fertile period.

The '29 Cord featured front-wheel drive. Ford put a V-8 in its '32, the first low-priced V-8. (It would be all alone in that market until Chevrolet and Plymouth got V-8s in 1955.) Pierce-Arrow, Lincoln and Cadillac experimented with V-12 and V-16 engines.

A number of makes used superchargers, which forced air into the carburetor to allow the engine to burn more fuel faster. The modern turbocharger is based on the same principle, but the turbocharger is driven by exhaust gas, not the engine.

In 1938, Oldsmobile offered Hydra-matic transmission as optional equipment, the first true automatic that worked.

The Depression also finally did in William Durant. About two months after his second and final ouster from General Motors in late 1920, Durant incorporated Durant Motors. He had no car, but he had the faith of investors and goodwill of dealers and before production began in 1921 of the Durant Four, he had 30,000 dealer orders. The next year, he brought out a low-priced car, the Star, to compete with Ford and Chevrolet.

Durant was on his way again. He added nameplates — the Flint, the Eagle, the Princeton and the Mason truck. To compete with Cadillac, Packard and Lincoln, he acquired Locomobile. He gobbled up supplier firms.

In 1927, he announced formation of Consolidated Motors, clearly intended to rival GM. It would include the Star, Moon, Chandler, Gardner, Hupmobile, Jordan and Peerless. But it never became a reality, because Durant was again in financial trouble.

A major figure in the bull market of the '20s, Durant had amassed a $50-million fortune by 1927, but displayed his old weakness of losing interest in day-to-day management of his company in favor of empire building and stock manipulation.

When the crash came in '29, Durant was hit hard. In 1933, Durant Motors went broke. He was down, but not out.

He still had a plant in Lansing and he signed a deal to build and market the Mathis, a small French car. But in the depths of the Depression, it never got off the ground. In 1936, William Durant filed in bankruptcy, claiming debts of $914,231 and assets of $250.

In 1940, he opened a bowling alley in Flint, the North Flint Recreation Center. Always thinking big, he had plans for 50 such centers across the country. He suffered a massive stroke in 1942, shortly after a trip to Nevada to investigate a venture in mining cinnabar, a mercury ore.

He and his wife moved to New York, where they lived quietly, supported in part not by the General Motors he had created, but by four long-time associates — C.S. Mott, R.S. McLaughlin, John Thomas Smith and Alfred P. Sloan.

Durant died in that apartment March 18, 1947.

When the Democrats nominated Al Smith to run for president in 1928, Smith called on a friend for help, John Jacob Raskob, chairman of GM's finance committee, and a lifelong Republican who described his profession in his Who's Who listing as "capitalist." Raskob accepted the job of chairman of the Democratic National Committee.

Sloan, an ardent supporter of Herbert Hoover, demanded that Raskob resign, either as Democratic chairman or from GM. Raskob refused. The board of directors supported Sloan in a split decision.

Hurt, Raskob resigned from GM. So did Pierre du Pont, board chairman and Raskob's mentor. Smith, of course, lost the race for the White House to Herbert Hoover.

After Raskob resigned, he cashed in $20 million worth of GM stock and built the Empire State Building, a spectacular, though unprofitable, undertaking. He continued as Democratic chairman, playing an important role in the election of Franklin D. Roosevelt as president in 1932 — an unusual role for a self-proclaimed "capitalist."

In Europe, the industry had taken a somewhat different path than the American, with U.S. companies generally leading in mass-production techniques. But the period between the wars were also fertile in Europe.

In newly created Czechoslovakia, Tatra began building unusual but high-quality cars in 1923. In Britain, Morris Garages began building the MG in 1924. The world's two oldest auto makers, Germany's Daimler and Benz, merged in 1926 to form Mercedes-Benz. In 1923, Opel became the first German maker to mass produce cars using American techniques, then was acquired by GM in 1928.

In 1927, a Swedish ball-bearing company named Volvo (Latin for "I roll") began building solid automobiles and in 1928 Bayerische Motoren-Werke began building a car called BMW. Citroen introduced its first front-drive model in 1934.

In Japan, DAT was building a second-generation car called Son-of-Dat, or Datson (the DAT stood for initials of the founders, Den, Aoyama and Takeuchi). The car's name was changed to Datsun in 1932 to tie in with the Rising Sun of Imperial Japan. Most of the Japanese nameplates familiar to the modern world did not yet exist.

And, in 1934, Adolf Hitler ordered Ferdinand Porsche to design a "People's Car," or "Volkswagen."

Top Above; "Battle of the overpass"

Right; Edsel Ford

UAW born amid sitdowns and battle of the overpass

On May 26, 1937, one of the most famous incidents in American labor history took place.

Walter Reuther, a former Ford employe fired for union activities, an executive board member of the fledgling United Auto Workers, and three colleagues were passing out union handbills on the pedestrian overpass near Gate 4 at the Ford Rouge plant.

They were seeking to organize Ford Motor Co., the auto industry's last citadel of resistance to the unions. With Reuther were Richard Frankensteen, a UAW vice-president, and two other union organizers, Robert Kanter and J.J. Kennedy.

They were approached on the overpass by several toughs, employes of Ford Motor Co. who worked for Harry Bennett, Ford's mysterious and sinister labor relations manager.

"This is Ford property," one of them informed the unionists. "Get the hell off here."

The four began to head for another stairway when the Ford men grabbed them and beat them bloody. Press photographers were there and got it all on film.

The incident became a *cause celebre* and entered the folklore of the labor movement. Frankensteen later ran unsuccessfully for mayor of Detroit. Reuther later successfully built the UAW into one of the most powerful unions in the world.

But "the battle of the overpass" didn't really have much effect on things. Ford would not be organized for another four years. And the most important strike in the organization of the auto industry had already taken place.

It wasn't supposed to happen the way it did. The UAW had

carefully prepared its assault on General Motors, by 1936 the largest auto maker in the world. It planned to strike in Flint. But it started in Cleveland.

Workers at GM's Fisher Body plant in Cleveland were angered when the plant manager refused to discuss reductions in the piece work rate. On Dec. 28, their representative walked down the line that made bodies for the nation's biggest-selling car, banging on the machines with a wrench and what he shouted would shock GM and the world before it was over: "Sit down! Sit down!"

The workers shut off the machines and sat down. They would not leave.

Two days later, members of the Flint UAW local seized the giant Fisher No. 1 and Fisher No. 2 plants. Within a week, GM was out of the auto-making business.

The strike was not rancorous. In fact, workers in Cleveland left the plant after GM promised not to try to reopen it until the strike in Flint was settled.

Early in 1937, GM went to court and asked for and received an injunction ordering the workers out of the plant and the pickets removed. But the union discovered that the judge owned $200,000 worth of GM stock. Embarrassed, GM dropped its request.

On Jan. 11, an uneasy truce which had prevailed in Flint was shattered when plant guards barred delivery of evening meals to the 100 men occupying Fisher No. 2 and a GM official turned off the heat in the plant.

Both sides called in reinforcements. Union toughs from Detroit — many recruited by the president of the Kelsey-Hayes UAW local, Walter Reuther, from Jimmy Hoffa's Teamsters local — headed for Flint. The Flint police headed for the plant.

Strikers seized the gate and police fired tear gas. The wind shifted and the police retreated under a hail of parts and debris thrown by the strikers. A few police drew their pistols and fired. Several workers were wounded, one seriously.

Michigan Gov. Frank Murphy, a liberal Democrat, ordered the National Guard into Flint, not to break the strike but to keep the peace. Hostilities ceased, the workers agreed to leave the plant, GM promised not to try to break the strike and not to try to resume production. Except for one hitch, collective bargaining had come to GM.

The hitch was a telegram William Knudsen sent to the Flint Alliance, an anti-strike group organized by GM officials, assuring that GM was ready to talk to "any group of employes" about any issues. He did it because he wanted so badly to get everyone back to work. But the union interpreted it as a double-cross and the workers stayed in the plant.

GM went to court again and got an injunction ordering the workers out. In response, workers seized the Chevrolet engine plant in Flint. Since there were no car bodies being made anyway, the action was purely symbolic, but it had the desired effect of raising worker morale and infuriating GM.

GM's rivals were building cars, GM was not. So GM agreed to negotiate and within a week, agreement was reached.

The strike, which lasted 44 days, was over. Fewer than 2,000 workers, acting in concert and quite illegally, had shut down GM and idled more than 150,000 other workers. The contract did not give the workers much. But the UAW was established.

In 1933, President Roosevelt signed the National Industrial Recovery Act, which ordered industries to work out standards governing operation, production levels, prices and working conditions. Henry Ford, calling the program's symbolic Blue Eagle "Roosevelt's buzzard," refused to sign the code, although most other auto makers did.

Henry's son, Edsel, president of Ford Motor Co., wanted to sign the code, but the old man refused. It was one of many conflicts between the father and son. Edsel had been president of Ford Motor Co. since 1919, but there was no question that Henry ran the show.

It is not easy, they say, to be a great man's son, but Edsel was also a top Ford executive, also a difficult role that few men played for long. William Knudsen, Harold Wills and Norval Hawkins were gone, all strong executives who found it impossible to work long for Henry Ford.

It fell to Edsel to convince the old man that the day of the Model T was over. The Model A, which replaced it, was a smashing success, but Henry never really forgave Edsel.

Henry Ford's view of his workers was paternalistic. After all, he had initiated the $5 day. But he did not really know what it was like to work in one of his auto factories. Edsel tried to tell him and Henry did not like it. He withdrew more and more from his son.

Edsel accomplished much at Ford despite this. He made Lincoln important in the luxury-car market and was the driving force in the elegant styling that marked

Ford cars in the '30s and in development of the Mercury line of cars.

As the gap between father and son widened, Henry came to rely more on Harry Bennett. He was fascinated with this ex-prize fighter's bizarre lifestyle and underworld connections.

Ford assigned Bennett to "mold" Edsel, to "toughen him up." (He didn't.) Edsel was stunned when Bennett was named labor relations manager and very nearly resigned from the company. (He didn't.)

The late '30s and early '40s were a difficult time for GM Chairman Alfred P. Sloan. The sitdown strikes of '36 and '37 disturbed him deeply. So did the Roosevelt administration — not only for what it did, of which Sloan greatly disapproved, but because it doggedly refused to heed his advice.

There were charges that high GM officials were sympathetic to the Nazis. Absurd now, in light of GM's outstanding contribution to the war effort, but disturbing then.

In a lawsuit brought by minority stockholders challenging the corporation's bonus plan, Sloan and other top administrators were ordered to forfeit millions of dollars. But what really galled Sloan was the judge's implication (erroneous) that nothing was done at GM without J.P. Morgan's approval.

In 1940, Nazi Germany invaded Denmark, thereby infuriating William Knudsen. Against Sloan's wishes, Knudsen resigned as president of GM to go to war against the Germans as chairman of the National Defense Council.

And in 1940, one of Sloan's closest friends, Walter P. Chrysler, died.

The UAW organized Ford in 1941. Again, it was not planned. On April 2, 1941, eight workers were fired at the Ford Rouge plant and 50,000 workers walked out in a wildcat strike. Workers blocked all entrances to the Rouge plant with an automobile caravan. They used Fords to shut down Ford.

A week later, Ford agreed to a National Labor Relations Board election. Henry Ford was deeply hurt when 97 percent of his workers voted for the union. In June, a contract was drawn up. Ford read it, thought about it and refused to sign it.

The Ford organizing strikes had been violent, with battles between strikers and Bennett's men, and between picketers and scabs. Henry's wife, Clara, was sick of the violence and envisioned more. She talked her husband into signing.

Henry Ford later explained to Charles Sorensen, the top executive who stayed with him the longest (40 years, until 1944, when he left to run Willys-Overland):

"I'm sure now she was right. The whole thing was not worth the trouble it would make. I felt her vision and judgment were better than mine. I'm glad that I did see it her way."

Through all this strife, cars continued to be changed and improved. In 1937, Pontiac moved the gearshift from the floor where it had always been to the steering column, a complicated change. (In the '60s, it would be moved back onto the floor in certain sporty models at extra cost.)

With the '38 models, Oldsmobile introduced the automatic transmission. Studebaker offered windshield washers and Buick introduced directional signals.

Ford introduced a whole new line of cars with the '39 models, the Mercury. Sealed-beam headlights first appeared on cars in '39, as did pushbutton radios. In 1940, Nash introduced the first mass-produced unitized body and Chrysler Corp. unveiled the safety-rim wheel. Packard offered the first air conditioner.

And in 1941, Chrysler became the first company in the world to mass-produce tanks, Ford built combat vehicles, GM turned out machine guns and antiaircraft guns, Studebaker accepted a contract for aircraft engines and Willys began delivering a quarter-ton four-wheel-drive vehicle to the Army which had been developed by American Bantam and would become known as the "Jeep."

The nation was deeply divided on Dec. 7, 1941. After 12 years of depression, high unemployment and labor strife, it was divided between haves and have-nots, rich and poor, labor and management. And it was deeply split on whether the United States should get involved in the war spreading throughout the world.

The Japanese healed those divisions with an attack on Pearl Harbor, which united this nation as it never had been before (or has been since).

On Dec. 8, all thought turned to the war effort. Conversion of the auto industry's industrial might to war production, already under way, intensified.

On Feb. 9, 1942, the last passenger car rolled off the line.

Rioters drag man from streetcar on Woodward.

World War II Jeep

War halts car production and forever changes U.S.

In the summer of 1940, the Army tested a small, lightweight vehicle developed by American Bantam Co., of Butler, Pa.

American Bantam began life as American Austin in 1930, but even in the depths of the Depression Americans did not like small cars and sales languished. Production ceased in 1935, then the company began building a very jauntily styled small car called the Bantam in 1937.

Jaunty or not, Americans still didn't care much for small cars. The Bantam, a collector's item now, did not sell well then. But the Army liked Bantam's little military vehicle and ordered 1,500 of them. Dubious of American Bantam's production capabilities, it placed similar orders with Willys-Overland and Ford Motor Co.

After rigorous tests and changes in specifications, Willys' version was standardized. But Willys could not satisfy the Army's voracious appetite and Ford was also appointed to build the vehicles, known in Army parlance as "vehicle, ¼-ton, GP (General Purpose)." The GP was quickly Americanized to "Jeep."

Willys did design and build the World War II Jeep version that was finally used and it got the rights to build civilian versions of it after the war. It was soon Willys' most successful vehicle. Later Jeep was acquired by Kaiser-Frazer, then by American Motors and it is now AMC's most successful vehicle.

But Bantam and the Army had laid the groundwork for the Jeep's success. American Bantam went out of business shortly before the war began.

Jeeps were just a fraction of the torrent of war materiel which poured from the auto industry.

Chrysler Corp. mass-produced

tanks and numerous makers built trucks for the military. The Army wanted to standardize its trucks to ease the parts and maintenance problem, but there was no time. Getting the trucks to the battlefields was more important.

An attempt was made to keep trucks of the same make together. Studebaker trucks, for example, were largely sent to allies under lend-lease and Russian auto men say there are still a few Studebakers in use in the vastness of the Soviet Union.

After civilian car production ceased in February, 1942, GM ordered its divisions to take any contract they could handle and to concentrate on the toughest tasks. GM built shells, bombs, fuses, navigation equipment, machine guns, artillery and anti-aircraft guns in addition to engines and vehicles.

One of Edsel Ford's last undertakings before he died (at 49, of a broken heart, claimed some romantics, although the proximate medical cause was undulant fever apparently brought on by drinking unpasteurized milk from the Ford dairy herd) was to oversee construction of the huge Willow Run plant which mass-produced bombers.

The auto makers more than doubled their productive capacity during the war and the influx of workers put the most severe pressures on the city in its long history.

(Visitors are often amazed to find that Detroit is older than many of the colonial cities in the East, founded in 1701 as a military post and trading center by Antoine de la Mothe Cadillac, a French adventurer and explorer who recognized the site as well suited for command of the lakes and well removed from the power of the French crown and church centered at the older post at Mackinac.)

Whites from Appalachia and blacks from the Deep South poured into the city and were jammed into already congested neighborhoods — the blacks into "Paradise Valley" on the near east side and Southern whites into the near west side. Woodward Avenue was the dividing line and, for a few days in 1943, a battlefield.

Many black families had settled here in the early 19th century, since Detroit was northern U.S. terminus of the "Underground Railroad" which moved runaway slaves from the South to the North and Canada. From these older families, a black middle class had grown, successful but separate. Racism ran deep.

In 1932, GM seriously considered dropping Cadillac, because

of the weak luxury-car market in the depths of the Depression. Nicholas Dreystadt, Cadillac service manager at the time, had noticed that the Cadillac was very popular with middle-class blacks, despite Cadillac's policy of not selling to blacks.

At an Executive Committee meeting called by Chairman Alfred P. Sloan to consider Cadillac's fate, Dreystadt made a surprise appearance with a scheme to save the car. Dreystadt was one of the last of the managers who rose to the top from the factory floor. He still spoke with a German accent, having immigrated to the United States in 1912 at the age of 13 as a member of a Mercedes racing team.

Dreystadt pointed out that since blacks (Negroes in those days) had limited access to high-status housing and other signs of success, wealthy blacks had adopted Cadillac as a status symbol. (Packard was the favored car of the white old-money class.)

Dreystadt pointed out that blacks paid a premium to white buyers to front for them. Demand like this should be exploited, he said. The committee give Dreystadt 18 months to develop the Negro market. By the end of 1934, Cadillac sales were moving up and the division was making money.

Dreystadt was not a civil rights crusader, but unlike many in the auto industry he drew no color line. So when as general manager of Cadillac during the war he accepted a contract to produce aircraft gyroscopes and skilled workers were simply not to be found, he startled the corporation by hiring and training 2,000 aging black prostitutes from Paradise Valley.

He and his personnel manager, James M. Roche, also hired their madams, reasoning plausibly enough that they could manage the women.

Dreystadt's unorthodox approach had often put him at odds with the professional managers who were increasingly taking over the auto industry, but this episode put him at odds with just about everyone.

In fact, the women did well and eventually surpassed their quotas. There were plenty of jokes about Dreystadt's "red-light district," but he did not think they were funny. At war's end, the women were let go because returning veterans had preference and the workers wanted them out of the plants.

Dreystadt felt he had personally failed these women (several reportedly committed suicide rather than return to their old lives) to whom he had given a taste of dignity and self-respect.

The riot started on a hot Sunday in July of 1943 with fights on Belle Isle between white and black youths and servicemen. It was over within the week, but before it ended the city witnessed a race riot as ugly as any in history, 35 people were known to have been killed and for the first time in the nation's history regular troops of the U.S. Army were used to halt a racial conflict. The next time they were used, in 1967, it would again be in Detroit.

The war plants — and the nation — needed workers and their color was unimportant. So was their sex. For the first time, women in large numbers entered the male-dominated work world and many of them liked it. In a very real sense, World War II gave the civil rights and feminist movements a powerful push.

It was not widely known, but Ford Motor Co. was near collapse. War work was keeping it going, but just barely. Henry Ford was still firmly in charge and his accounting procedures, cost controls and management systems were baffling to say the least. Goaded by Harry Bennett, the old man had fired most of his best executives. Only his son, Edsel, and Charles Sorenson were left and they held things together only by superhuman effort.

After Edsel died in 1943, the government was alarmed at the possibility of one of its biggest defense contractors collapsing, so it called Henry Ford II back from his post as an ensign in the Navy with the mission of saving the Ford empire.

Except for his name and the fact that he was the legendary man's grandson, Henry II had little to recommend him for the task. Based on his paper qualifications and credentials, he probably wouldn't have been hired for a responsible job by any personnel manager. Which shows how misleading paper qualifications can be, because young Henry did indeed save the empire.

Ironically, it was the end of the war that brought the crisis to a head. Ford costs were high and its product archaic, compared with the competition. Post-war demand for new cars would give the company a few years to reorganize, but there was no reason to think the old man would do it — or even agree that anything was wrong.

Once again, his wife Clara used her influence and pleaded with her husband to step aside. Edsel's widow Eleanor went even further, threatening to sell her stock unless the old man turned over the company to her son. In 1945,

Henry Ford gave in. Henry Ford II took over Ford Motor Co. Two years later, Henry Ford died.

The young man's first task was to wrest the company from Harry Bennett, who been virtually running Ford Motor Co. after Edsel died. Bennett had many talents, but running an automotive empire was not one of them. Henry II fired him. But Bennett did not leave.

John Bugas was an ex-FBI man who had was recruited to work for Bennett, but became a close confidant of young Henry. With his .38 inside his jacket, he went to Bennett's office. Bennett cursed him and took a .45 from his desk drawer and set it on the desk in front of him. He talked for a while. Bennett left his office, never to return.

Henry II quickly went to work to turn the company around. He responded to a peculiar telegram from Charles (Tex) Thornton, an Army Air Corps colonel, offering for employment a 10-man team of young officers who had run the Air Corps Office of Statistical control. Ford hired them.

They became known as the "whiz kids" and many worked their way to high positions in the company. While Thornton went on to head Litton Industries, two of them — Robert S. McNamara and Arjay Miller — became presidents of Ford Motor Co. McNamara, of course, went on to become secretary of defense in the Kennedy and Johnson administrations.

Henry II also hired a GM executive and Sloan favorite (apparently with Sloan's blessing), Ernest R. Breech, to preside over the turnaround. Breech served Ford well, reshaping it in the GM mold. The company was not yet out of trouble. But it was heading in the right direction.

If a car enthusiast found himself suddenly set down in the late '40s at Livernois and Grand River in Detroit, he might think he had died and gone to heaven. For miles in either direction, Livernois was a shining, chromed sea of new and used cars, the greatest auto row in history.

Passenger car production resumed with 1946 models, but with hundreds of thousands of men returning from the war, Detroit couldn't come close to meeting the demand. The dealers were suddenly in the driver's seat and many took advantage of the situation. The stereotype of the schlock-artist used-car dealer entered the American culture.

Used-car dealers became local celebrities with their flamboyantly aggressive sales tactics and their use of a fledgling advertising medium, television, to hawk their wares. Big-volume used-car dealers like Earl "Mad Man" Muntz in Los Angeles became public figures. Mad Man, who was immortalized as the butt of jokes by Bob Hope, later built TV sets and his own sports car, the Muntz. But building cars was much different than selling them and by his own admission Muntz lost about $1,000 a car.

Luckily, he didn't sell very many.

It was an exciting time in Detroit. The war was over and everyone wanted to get about the business of peace. (We would be back at war again in five years, but auto production was never again interrupted.)

In Europe, the auto plants were in ruins and there was no industry to speak of in Japan. American and British bombers blasted Opel and German Ford factories to rubble with equipment made by their American parent firms. The Russians stripped auto plants in Germany's Eastern zone of their machinery and such proud old names as Auto Union headed west along with the rest of the refugees. France nationalized Renault after Louis Renault, charged as a collaborator, died in prison.

But in North America, The plants were converting to civilian production, there was plenty of work and plenty of money. Families were being formed, the suburbs were being built, plans for a nationwide system of interstate highways were being seriously discussed and everybody wanted a car.

The auto industry was on the threshhold of its golden age.

Livernois Avenue's miles of used cars.

First postwar Ford rolls off assembly line in December, 1945.

The golden age: tailfins and dreams of glory

Most of the heroes of World War II were military men and political leaders, but one industrialist who became a hero was Henry J. Kaiser, who turned out Liberty Ships faster than German U-boats could sink them.

After the war, he decided to take on Detroit.

His new partner, Joseph Frazer, had worked for General Motors, Chrysler Corp. and Willys-Overland before picking up the failing Graham-Paige just before the United States entered the war. After the war, Frazer leased the giant Willow Run bomber plant that Ford had built and the team hired Howard Darrin (who made a reputation before the war styling very elegant custom Packard bodies) to design a car.

Kaiser and Frazer were not the only men with dreams of glory in that postwar automotive era when anything sold. There was William Stout and his Scarab, Gary Davis and his three-wheel Davis, Earl "Madman" Muntz and his Muntz sports car. They did not make it.

And there was Preston Tucker. His Tucker Torpedo was long and low, with an aluminum, air-cooled engine and a cyclops-like centered headlamp which turned with the front wheels.

Tucker raised about $25 million through the sale of stock and dealer franchises. It didn't last long. He built about 50 prototypes before his company collapsed, under attack from Drew Pearson on the radio and under investigation by the SEC.

Tucker went down even though Ed Cole, General Motors' premier engineer, said he thought Tucker's car was "well-conceived." But

Tucker found that $25 million was not enough to get in the game.

It didn't matter much what it looked like — anything sold after the war. Studebaker introduced the first post-war design in 1946, a radical, streamlined car with fenders integrated into the body and a distinctive wraparound rear window on its Starlite Coupe. Comedians made fun of it, claiming you could not tell if it was coming or going. But it sold well.

Kaiser-Frazer surprised everyone by leading all the independent makers in production in 1947, building 144,500 cars. Henry J. had done the impossible again. He had taken a seat in Detroit's high-stakes game.

Or so it seemed. By 1955, Kaiser-Frazer was gone (after an abortive effort to sell a small car called the Henry J through Kaiser dealers and the Allstate through Sears, Roebuck).

"We were not surprised that we had to toss $50 million into the automotive pool," Kaiser said later. "We were surprised that it disappeared without a ripple."

Hudson and Nash had merged into American Motors and Studebaker and Packard had joined forces. Soon Hudson and Nash both disappeared, replaced by Rambler, and the once proud name of Packard was affixed to some of the strangest-looking Studebakers ever made. Both Packard and Studebaker were doomed. The strategy conceived by Alfred P. Sloan and perfected by General Motors President Harlow Curtice in the '50s was working.

Sloan introduced the concept of "dynamic obsolescence" and annual model changes in the late '20s and early '30s as a way to increase demand for new cars to higher levels. It also raised the ante in the auto game. Smaller companies found it increasingly difficult to meet the expense of annual model changeovers.

After William Knudsen left his position of president of GM to head the nation's defense buildup in 1940, Charles Wilson was named president. Wilson was only 15 years younger than Sloan, but he was definitely of a different generation.

Wilson and Walter P. Reuther had developed a considerable amount of mutual respect, even friendship. Wilson saw that the workers wanted security. He began working out a plan for a guaranteed annual wage.

In the economic structure which Detroit had built, the laws of supply and demand had been modified. Largely because of GM's financial system, devised in the '20s by Sloan and his chief economic lieutenants Donaldson Brown and Albert Bradley, when sales dropped prices did not drop — the use of labor did. The financial risks inherent in the automotive sales cycle were shifted from stockholder to worker.

On Aug. 16, President Harry Truman lifted the wartime wage freeze, saying increases would be allowed, provided they did not force a price increase. The president had inadvertently given Reuther the issue he needed to battle GM and to win control of the UAW. As head of the GM unit of the UAW, Reuther asked for a 30 percent wage increase and demanded that GM open its books so all could see if the corporation could afford the increase without raising prices.

He knew, of course, that there was no way GM would do this. The UAW struck GM. The strike dragged on for months. In January, Ford and Chrysler settled for 18.5 cents an hour, a wage increase of 17.5 percent. Neither company agreed to hold down the price of its cars.

But Reuther insisted that GM hold down the price of its cars. And he insisted on an extra penny, "the frosting on the cake." Wilson refused. A month later, the UAW and GM signed a contract which raised wages 18.5 cents per hour.

Nothing was said about prices.

Reuther did not get his extra penny, nor did GM open its books. But the workers liked Reuther's style. They elected him president of the UAW.

The '48 Cadillac had small, attractive fin-like curves on its rear fenders to house its taillights. GM styling boss Harley Earl said he was inspired by the P-38, a twin-fuselage World War II fighter plane.

Eventually, other makers began putting tailfins on their cars. In one of the most curious styling fads in history — the fins had no function whatsoever except to sell cars — the fin became the symbol of the American car of the '50s, reaching bizarre proportions before it ran its course.

The '49 model year was the big one. All remaining prewar designs were swept away. Ford Motor Co. made its move. The '49 Ford, with fenders fully integrated into the body, was a classic statement of modern car design.

That same year, Chrysler took a wrong turn. It went for the old-fashioned virtues of solid construction, lots of headroom, functional styling. In short, the '49 Plymouths, Dodges, DeSotos and Chryslers were excellent, but dull.

Ford, which had lost the No. 2 sales position to Chrysler Corp. in the '30s, passed Chrysler in 1950. Chrysler was made permanently a small factor in the U.S. market after those comfortable, but stodgy '49 models.

At GM, meanwhile, Charles Kettering had one more major contribution. After the copper-cooled engine failure in the early '20s, Kettering took charge of GM's research operations. Over the years, GM Research Laboratories came up with numerous developments, none more important than tetraethyl lead.

Kettering's researchers discovered that adding tetraethyl lead to gasoline was an inexpensive way to increase octane and end engine knock, or pre-ignition. This allowed development of a more efficient higher-compression en-gine. (GM later spun off its tetraethyl operation to form Ethyl Corp.)

Kettering described such an engine in an SAE paper in the mid-'40s. It was introduced in the '49 Cadillac and Oldsmobile. Few remember it in the Cadillac, because it was Oldsmobile that made the engine famous. Olds called it the Rocket 88 and it was an instant hit.

The other makers followed during the '50s with their own high-compression V-8s, but GM built a strong sales lead during those years when it not only had the automatic transmission all alone, but the high-compression V-8 also.

Nash unveiled its new aerodynamic design, which it called "Airflyte." But more than its

aerodynamic design, the public noticed its resemblance to an upside-down bathtub and that was what stuck.

Packard built its last truly elegant (if pregnant) design from '48 to '50, then it went modern, then weird, then under.

Studebaker looked to aircraft for inspiration and came up with its famous bullet-nosed models of '50 and '51, very attractive in Starlite coupe form, resolutely odd as four-door sedans. For '53, Studebaker unveiled a classic coupe, generally credited to Raymond Loewy, although others including Virgil Exner, famous for the giant tailfins on late '50s Chrysler products, also claimed credit.

It was one of the most beautiful cars of the postwar era, both in its standard form and as the European-looking Hawk, but Studebaker

would not survive the '60s. The expensive model changes were bleeding it, as they did Kaiser-Frazer, Willys and Packard.

With GM in the lead, cars got bigger, more luxurious and more powerful through the '50s. But they also became more reliable, safer and easier to drive. The American car of the '50s was probably the best for the money in the world.

Critics labeled Detroit's products "insolent chariots," but the public loved them. In 1949, new-car sales of more than 4.8 million finally topped the old record set in pre-crash 1929 by almost a million units. In 1955, sales approached 7.2 million.

There were a few clouds, but the future looked bright from Detroit.

Insolent chariots unsafe at any speed

The American auto industry's golden age started with the end of World War II and it faded in the mid-'60s. Through the '50s and the early '60s, Detroit dazzled the world with a procession of cars that were reliable, luxurious, powerful, low-priced, often beautiful, always interesting.

Americans loved then and bought them in undreamed-of numbers.

There were hints of what was to come. Along with the good-humored cracks about Studebakers back in the '40s, Bob Hope and Jack Benny also joked about the smog in Los Angeles. Before the '60s ended, Detroit did not think they were funny.

Detroit was also coming under increasing fire as engines got more powerful and tailfins got bigger. Critics wanted more sensible, more economical smaller cars. Many servicemen returning from Europe brought back little Volkswagens, MGs, Triumphs and Porsches, strange-looking relics of the '30s.

Detroit had not ignored the small car. Both Ford Motor Co. and General Motors had plans at the end of World War II to build small cars. Harlow Curtice, president of GM through most of the '50s, explained why neither program came to pass: "You can take the value out much more rapidly than you can take the cost out."

At the end of World War II, American makers were invited to consider purchase of Volkswagen. Ford executives dismissed the idea, as did Chrysler Corp. One Ford executive put it this way: "You call that a car?"

While Ford and GM canceled their small-car programs — both of which had been quite advanced — Chrysler offered a smaller version of its '49 Plymouth and Dodge, which was a dud and was killed by '52.

The Crosley, Kaiser's Henry J and Allstate (marketed by Sears), the Nash Metropolitan, Willys Aero and Hudson Jet all came and went in the early '50s. But the VW, dubbed "the Beetle" by its owners and later by the importer, continued its steady and rapid sales growth.

In 1952, Charles E. Wilson resigned as GM president to become secretary of defense in President Eisenhower's administration. He had served GM well during the hectic war years and the post-war changeover. He had been a central figure in bringing labor peace to the industry. But he is remembered most for saying "what's good for GM is good for the country," a statement often cited as an example of corporate arrogance.

But that was not what he said. And what he did say was not out of arrogance but out of Wilson's old-fashioned patriotism.

At the confirmation he was asked if he could make a decision as secretary of defense in the interest of the nation if it were adverse to GM.

"Yes sir, I could," Wilson said. "I cannot conceive of one, because for years I thought what was good for our country was good for General Motors and vice versa. The difference does not exist."

Harlow Curtice, as general manager of Buick Division in the late '40s, was intrigued with a custom job Buick's chief engineer Ned Nickles had done on his car. The engineer had put four "portholes" on each fender with bulbs wired into the distributor so they would light sequentially as each of the engine's cylinders fired.

Curtice ordered the portholes put on all Buicks, but without the lights. They became Buick's trademark. Like tailfins, they had no function except to sell cars. Buick moved from its eighth rank in sales to challenge and displace Plymouth in third.

Curtice succeeded Wilson as president of GM in 1952 and the Buick portholes were an example of his uncanny ability to divine what the buying public would go for.

Ford Motor Co. demonstrated that despite all the scientific

research available, the odds are steep against a new car. It introduced the Edsel as a '58 model amid great hoopla. It was dropped in '60.

The Edsel has become a symbol of failure, but in fact Ford lost little but face. The production facilities used for the Edsel were sorely needed to meet demand for the Falcon, Ford's highly successful compact car. Had it not been for the Edsel, the Falcon could not have set a record as the biggest selling new car ever introduced.

The first rumbles of trouble came from dealers who were losing sales to imports. Many in Detroit dismissed the growing ranks of foreign car buyers as oddballs, flakes, college professors and leftists. But many of the dealers knew they were buyers with above-average incomes, many of whom owned more than one car. They were not all oddballs, they were trend-setters.

When George Romney took over the new American Motors in 1954, he ordered that the Rambler be revived and launched his famous crusade against Detroit's "gas-guzzling dinosaurs."

Detroit was not worried. It sold more cars in 1955 than it had in any year in its history. Then in 1956, sales slumped, but import sales doubled. Romney was convinced. So was Ed Cole, general manager of Chevrolet. He wanted to build a small car of unusual design and he did. But not quite the way he wanted.

The Big Three unveiled their "compacts" as '60 models — Ford Falcon, Plymouth Valiant and Chevrolet Corvair. The Falcon and the Valiant were very conventional, but the Corvair was all-new, revolutionary in many ways. Its air-cooled six-cylinder engine was in the rear of the car. And unlike Charles F. Kettering's copper-cooled engine of the '20s, it worked well.

There were compromises between Cole's original design and what GM top management approved for '60 introduction. Frederic Donner had succeeded the ebullient salesman Curtice as chairman. The financial people were taking over Detroit and not just at GM.

Tire diameter was cut, the aluminum engine was modified, the plush interior was downgraded and a $15 stabilizing bar was deleted from the suspension system.

A Chevrolet test driver rolled over the first prototype on the test track, admittedly at high speed. A Ford test driver also rolled one over. Word spread at Ford that the Corvair had problems. In high-speed turns, the rear end of the Corvair tended to lift or "jack" and the wheels tucked under. And because of the rear engine placement, the car tended to oversteer, that is, turn more sharply at higher speeds. Most America cars understeer, which means they make a wider arc when turning at higher speeds. The combination of jacking and oversteer made the Corvair handle quite differently from most cars.

The Corvair split GM deeply. When Semon "Bunkie" Knudsen, son of William Knudsen, was named general manager of Chevrolet in 1961 succeeding Cole, it is said that he insisted he be allowed to make some changes in the Corvair or he would quit the corporation. Knudsen installed the stabilizer bar on the '64 Corvair and approved design of a com-

pletely new suspension for the '65.

But before the fix was made, more than one million Corvairs had been sold and the car had come to the attention of a young Harvard Law School graduate named Ralph Nader. Nader had been handling insurance litigation in Hartford, Conn., and gathering information about auto accidents. In 1964, this austere, intense loner moved to Washington and set up shop as a self-appointed lobbyist for the public.

He served as unpaid consultant to a new Senate Subcommittee on Executive Reorganization, chaired by freshman Sen. Abraham Ribicoff, former governor of Connecticut and brother of a Ford dealer. Ribicoff decided to hold hearings on the federal government's role in auto safety. Among Detroit "celebrities" called to testify were GM

Chairman Frederic Donner and the new president, James Roche.

They were not prepared for the hostile grilling they received from Ribicoff and, in particular, Robert Kennedy. The brusque Donner and the grandfatherly Roche turned in a dismal performance.

Nader had collected an enormous amount of data about the Corvair and wrote a book, "Unsafe at Any Speed," an indictment of the auto industry in general and the Corvair in particular. By 1965, more than 100 lawsuits involving the car had been filed.

It came out that GM had hired a private detective to follow Nader and to try to "get something" on the crusader. But there was nothing and the public was outraged that mighty GM would put a gumshoe on the trail of this lone lawyer. The upshot was that Roche appeared again before a congressional committee and publicly apologized to Nader. It was a class act by Roche. It was also a painful humiliation for this honorable man.

The Corvair was dead. In his book Nader cited the suspension on the '65 Corvair as an example of excellent engineering, what Chevrolet should have done in the first place. But the damage was done. Sales plummeted and in 1969 the Corvair was quietly dropped.

It was not widely mourned at GM. The Chevrolet sales department had never liked it, many dealers didn't like it; it was an engineer's car.

The auto industry was making money and sales were strong as the '60s came to a close. But things had changed. The golden age was over. Detroit was on the defensive. America's love affair with the auto, some said, was on the rocks.

Dinosaur slayer falters; car guys vs. money men

Shortly after he took over as president of American Motors, George Romney told a stockholders meeting: "I am praying daily that this company will be a success."

Apparently stunned by his obvious sincerity, the audience was silent. Then it applauded, long and enthusiastically. Romney had that effect on people.

At a meeting of workers in Milwaukee, he blistered some of them whom he felt were letting the company down with their sloppy work and drinking on the job. "It must stop!" the angry Romney said. A few days later, he personally ordered the firing of a supervisor and four workers for drinking on the job. Milwaukee hailed his toughness.

Romney, who had worked for the Automobile Manufacturers Association and then joined Nash-Kelvinator in 1948, had a way of disarming people with his candor and honesty. It always seemed spontaneous and real. And it may have cost him a shot at the White House.

Nash-Kelvinator and Hudson Motor Car Co. merged in 1954, with George W. Mason as chairman and president. Before the year was out, Mason died and Romney, who had been executive vice president, became president.

With his vigorous, evangelistic style, Romney took on the auto establishment. He crusaded against Detroit's "gas-guzzling dinosaurs," urging Americans instead to go for AMC's "compact" Rambler. Rambler sales grew, as did sales of imports. Americans, it seemed, were indeed turning against the dinosaurs.

But Romney did not limit his activities to selling cars or his crusades to dinosaurs. He also crusaded for better government and formed Citizens for Michigan, which produced a plan for revising Michigan's tax structure and played a leading role in writing a new state constitution.

One of the key authors of the new constitution was George Romney and he built a political following which in 1962 propelled him into the governor's mansion.

The enthusiastic governor with the auto industry "can-do" approach quickly caught the attention of the national press and political king makers. After he was elected to his third term as Michigan governor in 1966, the pressure to seek higher office intensified. Interest mounted in Romney as Republican candidate for the '68 campaign. The Republicans fully expected to wrest the White House from the Democrats in that year of protest, rioting and unpopular war and Romney came under the increasing scrutiny of the national media.

Much was made over the fact that he was born in Mexico. His Mormon grandparents had fled to Mexico in 1885 when Congress outlawed polygamy and the U.S. Constitution says the president must be a "native-born" American. Another issue was his own Mormon religion and that church's policies toward blacks.

But the thing that seemed most damaging to Romney's White House ambitions was a statement he made on a broadcast talk show in answer to a question about why he had changed position on Vietnam and now opposed the war. Romney explained that he had been "brainwashed" during a tour of Vietnam and had since come to regard the war as a mistake.

In saying he had been brainwashed, Romney was probably reflecting the view of many Americans who felt they had been misled on the war. In time, many politicians in effect made the same admission. But they did not use that word. It was, perhaps, too candid and the word "brainwash" plagued him for years. It knocked him out of the presidential race.

Romney later served his country as secretary of Housing and Urban Development in the Nixon administration's first term. But that was after he came closer to the White House than any other automotive man ever had.

Alfred P. Sloan had been careful at GM not to let his financial people take over from the engineers, manufacturing people and sales people. It was a partnership and the pattern still is followed at GM: the chairman is usually a financial man, while the president is an "automobile man" or a "car guy."

But the financial people greatly increased their power after World War II and a tension built up between "money guys" and "car guys." When the balance got out of whack, there was trouble.

The change became most visible first at Ford Motor Co., but the takeover came first at Chrysler Corp.

When Henry Ford II hired the "whiz kids" in his successful effort to save his financially shipwrecked company, they were exactly what was needed. The corporate finances were a shambles after years of eccentric and even bizarre management by a failing old Henry and the enigmatic Harry Bennett.

Robert McNamara, Ed Lundy, Arjay Miller, Jim Wright and the other "whiz kids," along with a GM-oriented management team brought in by Ernest Breech, seemed to be just what Ford needed. Breech had headed Bendix Aviation, partly owned by GM. One of Sloan's favorites, it has been said that he went to Ford with Sloan's approval because Sloan felt Ford needed Breech and Sloan did not want to see Ford fail.

At Chrysler Corp., however, the takeover was more complete. After the death of Walter P. Chrysler in 1940, K.T. Keller, Chrysler's own man, continued as president until 1950, when he moved into the chairman's seat which had been vacant since Chrysler's death. He named as president a lawyer named Lester Lum "Tex" Colbert.

Keller died in 1956 and the corporation once more had no chairman, until Colbert ascended to that post in 1960. Chrysler was run as a kind of an old boy's operation and during the '50s a stockholder named Sol Dann claimed that Chrysler profits were being eroded because higher prices were being paid to suppliers than need be. The reason, he said, was that high-ranking Chrysler executives owned financial interests in these supplier firms.

The largest Chrysler stockholder was Consolidation Coal Corp., whose chairman, George Love, took an interest in Dann's charges and as a director he led a campaign to clean up Chrysler's act.

To help, he brought in Touche, Ross & Co. as outside auditors. He was impressed with the intelligence and integrity of one of the auditors, Lynn Townsend.

Meanwhile, Colbert moved into the chairman's spot in 1960 and it came as no surprise when he named one of his top executives and an old and close friend, William C. Newburg, as president. After two months, Newburg was fired amid charges of conflict of interest. Later, Newburg claimed that he was made the sacrificial goat in a massive coverup engineered by Colbert.

Newburg had long been a protege of Colbert and had followed Colbert up the corporate ladder at Chrysler. Their wives were close friends and the Colberts and the Newburgs lived only a few blocks from each other. Colbert knew all about his holdings in a supplier firm. In fact, Newburg said, Mrs. Colbert inquired about the possibility of Newburg getting her son a summer job at his supplier firm.

Colbert and Newburg tried to avoid each other, but they traveled in the same social circles and they met the following year at a wedding reception at the Bloomfield Hills Country Club and exchanged a few heated words. Colbert left, then returned to the club in the afternoon. He encountered Newburg in the locker room. Onlookers say there were more words, then ex-lumberjack Newburg took a punch at ex-cotton trader Colbert. Friends say Colbert showed up the next day to play golf with a bandage on his chin, hiding the cut and stitches.

Colbert retired later that year and Love took over the corpora-tion as chairman, bringing in Townsend as his president and thus annointed him as his successor. Love stepped aside in 1966 and Townsend became chairman. Townsend recruited John J. Riccardo from Touche, Ross, making him president in 1970.

Chrysler was now run by financial people. Closest "car guy" to the top was Robert McCurry, a former Michigan State football star who was a favorite with the dealers. He left for Toyota.

While financial people were calling the shots everywhere now, the other makers all had "car guys" at the top also; Lee Iacocca at Ford (and Henry II himself was no mean judge of autoflesh); Ed Cole and Elliott "Pete" Estes at GM; Bill Luneburg at American Motors.

In Detroit, financial people could also be "car guys." But everyone knows what the terms mean — financial people put money first. The result at Chrysler Corp. and later in the '70s at Ford Motor Co. and General Motors was a selection of cars that the public didn't think looked so good. Not as good as what was coming out of Europe. Or out of Japan.

Iacocca and the
First Mustang

DeLorean and the '69 GTO

After the muscle cars, the world comes to an end

An outlaw auto culture took shape in the United States after World War II.

A generation of young people who came of automotive age in the postwar period were building an underground car culture based on speed and customized older cars they called "hot rods."

Marketing people say cars make a statement about their owners, the Chevrolet sedan as surely, albeit differently, as the Duesenberg. Detroit was not sure what to make of the statement posed by a chopped and leaded pearlescent purple '39 Mercury with frenched headlights and a "souped-up" V-8. So it ignored it. For a while.

Fords of the '30s and early '40s vintage were the most popular machines with the hot-rodders, because they were inexpensive and they had V-8 engines. Hybrids were not unusual. In the middle and late '50s, high-compression Chevrolet V-8 engines became popular and a '34 Ford with a Chevy V-8 and Hydra-matic drive (this was not the sports car crowd) was and is highly prized.

They cruised the growing number of drive-in restaurants and they blocked off little-traveled roads in the country — or in the cities — to race wheel to wheel with their high-powered rods.

Detroit ignored them for a while, but soon drag racing and stock-car racing became respectable and attracted wide followings. And these fans bought cars. Detroit wooed them with "muscle cars," factory hot rods.

Many critics disapproved of this outlaw band of auto lovers, but they became a part of American culture. They were too big a chunk of the generations now ranging from 35 to 60 to ignore. After pretending they were not there for about 20 years, Detroit began building cars for them in the '60s.

There were earlier attempts at appealing to the performance market. In '53, Chevrolet unveiled its Corvette, a beautiful fiberglass-bodied sports car which pleased hardly anyone. It had a ho-hum six and automatic transmission.

Ford's Thunderbird, introduced as a V-8 two-seater for '55, was better received, but there were plenty of back-alley artworks that would blow its doors off.

Over the years, the Corvette became a truly world-class sports car, while the Thunderbird swelled up into a luxury car. Both were priced well out of the ordinary car range.

In April, 1964, Lee Iacocca, then general manager of Ford Division, became the first person to appear on the covers of both Time and Newsweek magazines the same week. (Only Bruce Springsteen and Andrew Wyeth's model Helga have matched that feat since.)

Iacocca became famous that year because of the Mustang, a car that caught America's fancy as few have before or since. Ford hoped to sell 100,000 in its first year. In fact, 420,000 were sold in the first six months, shattering the former first-year mark set by the Ford Falcon in 1960.

The Mustang, itself an answer to Chevrolet's successful Corvair Monza, which showed there was a market for a small, inexpensive sports car, spawned a series of "pony cars."

The Mustang far outstripped the Corvair, because its V-8 engine far outstripped the Corvair's six. (Interestingly, in its efforts to get more power out of its air-cooled, rear-mounted six, Chevrolet fitted some Corvairs with turbochargers, foreshadowing present-day high-performance efforts.) The Mustang was offered with a big V-8 that would leave most cars in its exhaust. It was a factory hot rod.

And Iacocca rode it (with a few detours) to the presidency of Ford Motor Co.

Marlboro cigarets are a marketing textbook case of a turnaround in a product's image. From a low-volume ruby-tipped woman's cigaret, Phillip Morris and a tattooed cowboy made Marlboro into a macho brand and in a relatively short time it was the biggest-selling cigaret on the market.

The auto industry has its own "Marlboro story." It started in

1956, when General Motors President Harlow Curtice surprised the industry by naming Semon E. (Bunkie) Knudsen, a young (40), ambitious engineer and son of the legendary William Knudsen, to head the ailing Pontiac Division.

Pontiac had become a stodgy car with limited market appeal, a car for conservative old men and little old ladies. Knudsen decided the car needed a more exciting image and that the best way to do that was to, in fact, make the car more exciting.

When Marlboro went macho, Phillip Morris changed the formula of the cigaret's tobacco so that, in fact, it had a stronger, richer flavor that appealed to both men and women. And Knudsen decided to back up Pontiac's new image with an exciting car.

To help him do this, he hired an even younger engineer with plenty of ideas and ambition to match Bunkie's — John Z. DeLorean.

DeLorean, not yet 30, was an engineering boy wonder, first at Chrysler Corp., then at Packard, where he was head of research and development. Knudsen offered him a similar post at Pontiac.

Knudsen, his chief engineer, Elliot (Pete) Estes, and DeLorean secretly launched a stock-car racing activity — secretly because GM had agreed in 1955 along with the rest of the industry not to engage in factory racing efforts.

In the early '60s, a buyer or a dealer who knew what to look for in the Pontiac catalog of optional equipment could put together a racing machine, a factory hot rod.

In 1963, a dealer in Royal Oak, Ace Wilson, began marketing — with the help of Jim Wangers, of Pontiac's ad agency, MacManus, John & Adams — a hot rod made of stock Pontiac options. He called it the Bobcat. Part of the Bobcat package was the name, made up of rearranged letters from Pontiac model names and affixed to the car to let the world know that the owner had something special.

The Bobcat was both a financial and esthetic success and in its Tempest form it was the prototype of the Pontiac GTO, which came out in '64, just beating the Mustang to become the first "muscle car."

The GTO was the ultimate muscle car, the car all succeeding muscle cars would be judged by. Ironically, the GTO administered the coup de grace to the old-fashioned hot rod, because very few individuals could build one as cheap or as fast as the GTO. Only Ford and Chrysler Corp. had the resources to challenge it. And they did.

Estes later became president of

GM and Knudsen and DeLorean probably would have also, if they had not become impatient and quit GM.

When the GTO and the Mustang hit the market, gasoline was cheap. But the muscle cars would be on the way out before the first oil crisis in the early '70s, killed not because of the abandon with which they gulped fuel, but because smog and the toll of highway death and destruction were changing American attitudes toward the car.

Researchers in California had determined that the irritating cloud of smog that was spreading over not only the Los Angeles area, but metropolitan areas around the country, was caused by unburned hydrocarbons (droplets of gasoline) in automotive exhaust reacting with oxides of nitrogen, also present in auto exhaust, and sunlight.

California led the way in setting standards for air pollution and the effort to clean up auto exhaust drained Detroit's engineering resources starting in the mid-'60s until the new car was pretty well removed as a major source of air pollution a decade later.

But that enormously complex technological challenge wasn't the auto industry's only problem. When Ralph Nader did in the Corvair he showed that the auto establishment was not invulnerable and safety critics launched their own assault on the automotive citadel.

In fact, safety had long been a concern in Detroit. All were agreed that cars should be safer. The question was how best to do it.

Motorists and their passengers are killed and injured in automobiles not by the primary crash but by the so-called "second impact." When the car decelerates rapidly, as it does when it hits a tree, occupants continue to move forward, into the dashboard, the windshield, or the steering column to be bashed, decapitated or impaled.

To prevent or mitigate these second impacts, the auto makers installed seat belts, collapsible steering columns and safety windshields in their cars before the government enacted any standards. But the government said it had to do more.

In the late '60s, Eaton Corp. showed a system it had developed for aircraft which sensed a crash and inflated "air bags" into which the passenger would be thrown and cushioned from the hard surfaces inside the car.

The government and the insurance industry liked the air bags because many drivers declined to buckle up the belts that were standard equipment on all new cars starting in the mid-'60s. The auto makers didn't like them because of the space-age technology which they said could not be made fail-safe in a production-line operation. The belts work, Detroit said, make use of them mandatory.

Before the Organization of Petroleum Exporting Countries cut off the supply of oil to the United States in 1973 — by then imports accounted for some 40 percent of consumption — warnings were being sounded at industry meetings and in trade journals about the crisis to come. The United States was at the mercy of OPEC, they said, and over the longer range the world was running out of oil.

The government began setting fuel economy standards which were often in conflict with the air pollution and safety standards which had to be met.

Cutting nitrogen oxide emissions required making engines run less efficiently, thereby increasing fuel consumption. Making cars smaller to meet economy requirements often conflicted with safety designs. And some safety standards added weight to the cars, cutting fuel economy.

And when OPEC created a sudden demand for small, fuel-efficient cars in the mid-'70s, the American makers were not ready with good designs.

The Japanese were.

Japan first came into the United States in 1958 with the strange little Toyota Toyopet and Nissan Datsun. But the cars were second-rate and there was no sound dealer network to service them.

Nissan and Toyota withdrew. But they would be back. They studied American methods. And when they came back, they did it right.

Volkswagen was the first to feel the Japanese onslaught. VW had dominated import sales since it first started coming into the United States around 1950. But Toyota steadily closed the gap and passed VW in sales in the United states in 1975 and Nissan passed it the following year.

The Japanese had similar success against American nameplates. By the end of the decade, Japanese makers were selling 2.5 million cars a year in the United States, close to one in every four sales.

Detroit was reeling.

Malcolm Bricklin

Saviors of the industry: more dreams of glory

In the 1970s, the outside world crashed in on Detroit. Washington began telling it how to build cars and Middle East politics put the fear of gasoline shortages into America.

Washington, in its search for solutions to the knotty problems of air pollution, safety and fuel economy, stirred hopes anew of men who would build their own cars in defiance of the automotive establishment. As is often the case with intractable problems, public relations played a major role.

Difficult challenges confronted the auto industry and many private inventors tried to meet them. Washington, ever distrustful (with some reason) of the auto industry, encouraged newcomers and rekindled dreams of glory.

Many congressmen preferred to believe an unknown inventor who told them his steam car would work and would solve the air pollution problem rather than General Motors engineers who said the physical laws which set limitations that made steamers die out in the '20s were still there.

It is significant that despite all the interest in exotic engines, the cars that were actually built by independents were quite conventional.

And one of these conventional (in its power train, not its appearance) cars that created quite a stir was built by a most unconventional auto maker, Malcolm Bricklin. Before his dream of building a car with his own name on it ended in a flurry of legal actions in late '75, some 2,875 of the sleek safety/sports cars were built.

Of these, 790 were '74 models, powered with American Motors V-8s. For '75, Bricklin shifted to Ford V-8s and 2,083 of that model year were built. Only two '76 models had rolled off the line in New Brunswick when Bricklin Canada defaulted on loan payments and was placed in receivership.

Malcolm Bricklin was not a typical auto executive. He favored blue jeans and cowboy boots and came on more as a high-rolling gambler than a smooth Wall Street type. Nonetheless, he managed to raise more than $20 million to build the Bricklin.

A college dropout, Bricklin made his fortune in the retail hardware business. He started with three small A-frame stores, turned to franchising and within two years sold his interest in the 174-store Handyman chain for $1 million. He was not quite 22.

He went to work for Innocenti, an Italian firm which had a 15-year supply of Lambretta motors scooters sitting on lots in the United States (30,000 of them, with sales of 2,000 a year). "I sold 'em all in 60 days," Bricklin said.

He began distributing the Rabbit, a scooter built by Fuji Heavy Industries. Just as Bricklin was starting to roll, Fuji quit making the Rabbit. Bricklin went to Japan to try to persuade Fuji to change its mind. He had no luck with the Rabbit, but Fuji officials showed him the Subaru 360 and tried to interest him in selling the odd little car in the United States.

In 1968, Bricklin formed Subaru of America and was in the auto business. He stayed with the company until it went into the black in 1971. He kept his 9 percent interest, but left management to build his own car.

With a design for a low, sleek sportster with gull-wing doors, Bricklin raised more than $20 million and acquired an almost-new plant in St. John, New Brunswick.

When production began in 1974, the car was not quite what Bricklin had intended. It had a V-8 instead of a four and it cost $7,500, not "less than $3,000" as had been the goal. But one of Bricklin's highest priorities was that it look like a world-class car. It did.

After production ended, the price of Bricklin cars was quickly bid up to $11,000 and more. It was a popular car with its fans, but the maker went bankrupt.

Bricklin got back into the auto business after Fiat pulled out of the United States. He began importing the Fiat Spider 2000 as the Pininfarina and the X-1/9 as the Bertone. But these cars had not sold well as Fiats and their new names made no difference.

Then Bricklin started a company to import the Yugo, a warmed-over Fiat model built by Zastava in Yugoslavia, which has stirred up a great deal of public interest. Why did the Yugo capture the public's imagination while the much more elegant Pininfarina and Bertone have not? The Yugo's advertised price started at $3,990.

A number of other entrepreneurs tried to start their own auto firms in the '70s, the most famous of whom played a role in another interesting feature of the late '60s and early '70s, which was a series of top-level job changes.

When John Z. DeLorean left GM in 1973 as vice-president and group executive in charge of all car and truck divisions, he was following in the footsteps of his mentor at GM, Semon (Bunkie) Knudsen. Son of William E. Knudsen, a legendary automotive pioneer at both Ford Motor Co. and GM, Bunkie reversed his father's direction and left GM to go to Ford.

After making his name as general manager of Pontiac Division, during which time Pontiac changed its image from stodgy to hot, Knudsen moved rapidly to general manager of Chevrolet, then group vice-president and member of the board of directors and finally executive vice-president in charge of just about everything. He was on the fast track to the top.

But in 1967, Ed Cole was named president. Knudsen didn't like it.

About that same time, Henry Ford II had decided to head the National Alliance of Businessmen at the urging of President Lyndon B. Johnson. On Feb. 1, 1968, Knudsen quit GM and four days later became president and, in Henry's absence, chief executive officer of Ford Motor Co. His name was not on the building, but after Henry, Bunkie was boss. Iacocca, the heir apparent, was not amused.

Knudsen made a mistake that Iacocca did not make later when he went to Chrysler Corp. When Knudsen went to Ford, he did not bring (with a few exceptions) his own team from GM.

Ford executives quite naturally resented Knudsen coming in at the top. And they worked for Iacocca, who was then head of North American Operations.

Less than two years later, Ford fired Knudsen with a classic, if laconic, explanation: "It just didn't work out."

Fifteen months later, Iacocca was named president of Ford Motor Co. In 1978, he was fired by Henry. Once again, "it just didn't work out." By the time Iacocca got the ax, Chrysler Corp. was in deep trouble and in danger of going bankrupt. Chrysler Corp.

Chairman John J. Riccardo hired Iacocca and the auto maker was out of the hands of the accountants and back in the hands of auto men.

Iacocca went to work on Chrysler's uninspired product line and breathed new life into it. He went to Washington and sold Congress on the idea of loan guarantees for Chrysler to help it raise the capital it needed to compete; Chrysler needed new models because the system of dynamic obsolescence Alfred Sloan built was still operating.

There was much talk about "bailouts" and "corporate welfare," but the guarantees did not cost the taxpayers a cent and undoubtedly helped save Detroit's largest employer. They also helped make Lee Iacocca a hero, bigger than Henry J. Kaiser or George Romney had been in earlier days, a hero whose name is bandied about as a presidential candidate.

Bricklin and DeLorean were not the only would-be car makers in this new wave of automotive messiahs.

William Lear, of Lear jet fame, tried a number of times to develop a workable steam car, but never got it off the ground.

Wallace Minto devised a steam-er which used fluorocarbon fluid instead of water and interested Nissan in it. But it never saw production.

Sam Williams tried valiantly with turbines and put a few in American Motors cars.

The most bizarre episode was the attempt by Liz Carmichael, a six-foot 200-pound transsexual born Jerry Dean Michael, to build a three-wheeled car called the Dale.

The Dale, designed by Dale Clifft, was to be powered by a two-cylinder engine, get 70 mpg and sell for under $2,000. A sleek prototype was built, but production never began.

At Carmichael's trial on charges of grand theft, fraud and securities violations, Clifft said he still believed in Liz Carmichael. He claimed he stood to receive $3 million in royalties once the Dale went into production. In all, he received $1,001, plus a $2,000 check which bounced.

Carmichael went to prison.

The man who came the closest to success, the man who seemed to have everything it took to do it, was John Z. DeLorean.

His car was to be a gull-wing safety/sports car with Lamborghi-ni-like styling — similar in concept and looks to the Bricklin. ItalDe-sign helped with styling and Colin Chapman, of Lotus fame, was called in to help with engineering.

With financing from dealers, celebrities and the British government, DeLorean began production in 1980 in a plant in Northern Ireland. Within 17 months, the plant was closed. Fewer than 9,000 cars were built.

The DeLorean saga took a bizarre turn in 1982 when he was arrested in Los Angeles and charged with drug dealing. The government had the deal on videotape, but DeLorean was acquitted. Creditors and federal agents continued to try to track down millions of dollars they believe are hidden in the tangle of DeLorean organizations.

DeLorean's story is not over. And he still, from time to time, professes dreams of building his car.

In the '70s, the American love affair with the auto seemed to go sour. After the second oil crisis in 1979 caused a large and rapid increase in the price of gasoline, buyers wanted small cars and the Japanese had the best.

Detroit had been devoting most of its attention to meeting federal requirements in air pollution and safety and downsizing its traditional big-American-car offerings. The U.S. makers had done little to make their cars attractive to

buyers, an area in which they had led the world in the '50s and '60s. The Japanese had done much.

In the early '70s, sales soared to new heights. In 1973, sales of American-built cars totaled almost 9.7 million units, a record which still stands. That was the peak. Sales slid, while the Japanese, who had been working hard on making their cars attractive to the American buyer who wanted a small car, sold more and more cars in the United States.

Detroit seemed dispirited. Chrysler Corp. was sliding toward financial disaster. American Motors was in deep trouble. General Motors seemed to have lost its touch. It plowed $50 million into development of the Wankel rotary engine, but couldn't get it to work. Japanese maker Mazda did. Before the end of the decade Ford Motor Co. was losing money at an alarming rate and there was talk, unbelievable as it sounded, of Ford pulling out of North America.

America's love affair with the auto was being sorely tested. After the first oil crisis in '73, many people dumped their big American cars and took a beating. The crisis faded, big cars came back and the little cars they had bought were not worth much. They took another beating. The second oil crisis convinced everyone and Detroit phased out the big car and the big V-8 engine. But the car prices climbed. Buyers took another beating.

Skyrocketing oil prices caused economic recession, while government policy encouraged inflation. Cars, which Americans had taken for granted for decades, were becoming too expensive to buy, own and operate. At least American cars were.

But the Japanese offered a wide array of small, high-mpg and high-quality models. Detroit had concentrated on numbers, while Japan had concentrated on quality. The result was that the Japanese were selling about one of every four cars sold in the United States.

There were others in the '70s who would save the industry. Constantinos Vlachos, of Grand Couleee, Wash., developed an engineless car, which operated on fluorocarbon fluid vaporized by electricity from a battery, providing a high-pressure gas to operate pumps which rotated each wheel.

Frederick M. Guilfoyle, London, Ont., proposed to build a car powered by an fuelless engine with two-way pistons operated by compressed air. The air would be compressed by windmills.

Fortunately, problems were solved by more conventional means and eventually OPEC fell into disarray.

Japan's sun rising as new world becomes one

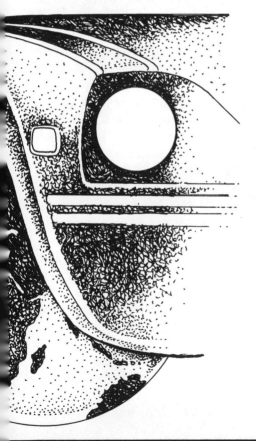

"Buy American," bumper stickers exhort us. Some take a more strident approach, inviting us to buy a Japanese car and put various numbers of Americans out of work.

But in fact, these are calls to the past. The internationalization of the auto industry is not something to be resisted. It has already happened.

While statesmen and diplomats claim they want to unite the world in brotherhood (or something) then work to keep the world divided, the auto makers have already moved a long way toward a one-world auto industry.

There is an increasingly blurred line between what is an American car and what isn't. Many cars assembled in the United States contain major components, such as engines or transmissions, made in other countries. Some cars made in other countries are sold with American nameplates. And some cars with foreign nameplates are assembled in the United States.

Is a car built in England by an American company American or English? Is a car built by a Japanese company in the United States Japanese or American?

The sixth Ford built in 1903 was sold to a Canadian buyer. And in 1904, Ford of Canada was founded in Windsor.

Ford began building cars in England in 1911, Brazil in 1919 and in Germany and Australia in 1925. Ford now assembles cars in Argentina, Ireland, Malaysia, Mexico, New Zealand, the Philippines, Spain, South Africa, Taiwan, Uruguay and Venezuela.

General Motors was a little slower moving into the international market, but it acquired a Canadian subsidiary in 1918, then took over the Vauxhall company in Great Britain in 1925. (Vauxhall was started in 1903, using as its symbol the Griffin, half-lion, half-eagle. It was named after the suburb of London in which it was located, which was in turn derived from a 12th century mercenary known as Fulk le Breant. Through marriage, he acquired a house on the River Thames, which became Fulk's Hall, later corrupted into Vauxhall. The griffin was Fulk's symbol.)

In 1929, GM acquired the Adam Opel company, one of Germany's oldest auto makers, then bought Holden's in Australia in 1931. GM also assembles cars in Europe, Asia and Africa and, in a joint venture with Toyota, it assembles Japanese cars in the United States.

Chrysler Corp. was forced to sell off its overseas holdings (Rootes Group in Great Britain and Simca in France) during its crisis of survival in 1979-82. Chrysler no longer owns Simca, which is now part of the Peugeot-Citroen group and builds the Talbot car, but its durable Omni/Horizon was in large part a product of Chrysler designers in France.

American Motors is itself almost half owned by Renault, which in turn is owned by the French government, seized during World War II after Louis Renault died in 1944 after he was jailed as a Nazi collaborator. AMC also builds the uniquely American Jeep in 19 countries around the world.

In the clamor for protection against Japanese cars that has built up in the last few years in the United States, General Motors and Ford Motor Co. have stayed firmly in the free-trade camp. They are and have been for most of their corporate lives multinational organizations.

Chrysler Corp. has hedged its

bet by selling Japanese cars and trucks under its own nameplate and now GM is doing the same.

Since the Reagan administration is against tariff protection for any industries and the auto industry has surprisingly little clout in Washington for such a big industry (most of its political successes have been with the help of its dealers; the National Automobile Dealers Association is one of the most effective lobbies in Washington), trade barriers to protect Detroit seem unlikely. The wave of the future may be more agreements such as the U.S.-Canada Automotive Trade Agreement, which by allowing duty-free trade at the wholesale level has, in effect, made the two nations a single market and allowed U.S. and Canadian makers to coordinate production and achieve greater economies.

Europe was where the automobile was born a century ago and many of its very earliest nameplates are still around, including those of Benz and Daimler (1886), which merged in 1926 to form Daimler-Benz, maker of the Mercedes.

There was also an English Daimler car, started in 1896. It was formed to produce Daimler cars under license and Gottlieb

Daimler was a director for several years, but the British and German firms went their own ways over the years.

In France, Peugeot dates back to 1890 and Renault to 1898. In Italy, Fiat was started in 1899 and other early British nameplates were Rolls-Royce and Rover (1904) and Austin (1906).

Czechoslovakia's best known car, the Tatra, was launched in 1897, long before Czechoslovakia existed (it was part of the Austro-Hungarian empire). It was called the Nusselsdorf, after the town where it was built. The name was changed to Tatra (a mountain range on the Czech-Polish border) after Czechoslovakia was created with Nusselsdorf within its territory.

But while the game began in Europe, the United States picked up the ball early in this century and ran with it.

Developments such as mass production, the moving assembly line and interchangeability of parts were pioneered here in Detroit by Ransom E. Olds, Henry Ford and Henry Leland. Mass production did not really come to Europe until the '20s, when Opel began adapting American techniques and Andre Citroen started building a "car for the masses."

The self-starter put the United States in the technological lead in car design, a position it held through development of the automatic transmission, various power accessories and low-cost powerful engines until the early '70s, when Japan took it.

"Made in Japan" used to mean "cheap imitation" and second-rate quality to most Americans until the '50s — the Korean war, to be specific, where photographers first noticed that Japanese lenses were as good or better than German and about half the price. Now "made in Japan" means high tech and high quality. Better than one in five cars sold in the United States are made in Japan. And most Japanese makers are building cars here in the United States or planning to.

A Japanese nameplate, the Mazda, is the only car in the world to be successfully marketed with a Wankel rotary-piston engine. The Germans, famed for their engineering, tried it and failed. In fact, Felix Wankel himself tried to perfect the engine for NSU, but troublesome problems remained.

General Motors, no slouch at engineering, spent $50 million on development of the rotary engine, but gave up on it before ever getting close to the marketplace.

Another Japanese car maker, Honda, was the first in the world to market a car with a stratified-charge engine.

And Isuzu has said it plans soon to market a passenger car equipped with a ceramic engine. Isuzu has succeeded in the industrial use of a ceramic engine, which is lighter that the conventional metal one and more fuel efficient. The new engine will have piston rings and valves and other combustion parts made entirely of ceramics, the company said.

The announcement of the ceramic engine came shortly after GM increased its holdings in Isuzu from 34.2 percent to 38.6 percent.

And in sheer numbers, the Japanese industry has challenged and surpassed the U.S.in production. This is impressive progress for an industry that did not take shape until after World War II.

Japanese firms were building cars early in the century, but its industry could not be compared with the European or American. The first car built in Japan was put together in 1902, but most of the Japanese makers began producing cars in the '50s and '60s.

The exceptions are the two biggest, Toyota and Nissan.

In 1912, Kwaishinsha Motor Car Works began work on an experimental car, which was put into production in 1914. It was called the Dat, derived from the initials of the partners, Den, Aoyama and Takeuchi.

In 1926, Kwaishinsha merged with another company to form Dat Automobile Manufacturing Co. With a name like Dat, oddly enough, it quit building the Dat and began making a car called the Lila. Then it got out of the car business entirely and built only trucks until 1930. Dat returned to car assembly in 1931 with the Son-of-Dat, or Datson. This was changed in a burst of nationalism in 1932 to Datsun, to tie in with the Rising Sun.

The company became Nissan Motor Co. in 1933. The Datsuns of the '30s were built in a full range of body styles and were based closely on the British Austin Seven.

Most Japanese cars of this era were copies of American or European models. After World War II, the '48 Datsun looked like an American Crosley and a British-looking sports car was added in 1952.

Toyota Automatic Loom Works began experimenting with cars in 1935. Its first cars looked remarkably like the Chrysler Airflow. During World War II, Toyota built a car that was a dead ringer for the last pre-war Plymouth.

The Toyota company was owned by the Toyoda family. The slight change in name was made because the family thought Toyoda was more difficult to pronounce. Americans, of course, pronounce both the same.

Both Toyota and Nissan began exporting cars to the United States in 1958, when sales of Datsun totaled 1,003 and Toyota's Toyopet 919. Both nameplates drifted without making much of a dent in the U.S. market. In fact, the cars were not right for the U.S. market and the Japanese pulled back to study the situation and retrench.

They studied American marketing techniques, built up sales and service networks, designed cars to appeal to U.S. buyers and began to move up in the sales charts in the late '60s.

Isuzu made its appearance in the U.S. market in 1966, but faded within a couple of years. Isuzu returned in 1976 in the guise of GM's Opel. GM had halted import of its German-built Opel and in 1976 began marketing a smaller Isuzu under the Opel name through its Buick dealers. Isuzu now markets its own cars in the United States.

In 1969, the Subaru made its U.S. debut. Built by Fuji Heavy Industries, it was introduced by Malcolm Bricklin, who is now bringing in the Yugo by Zastava of Yugoslavia.

In late 1970, two more Japanese nameplates appeared in the United States, Honda and Mazda.

The Mazda is manufactured by Toyo Kogyo, an unlikely firm to beat the automotive giants in development of the rotary piston Wankel engine, but it did. It was originally involved in manufacture of cork products and did not produce cars until 1960.

One of the first commercially manufactured cars in Japan was the Mitsubishi Model A, built from 1917 to 1921 and modeled after a Fiat of that period. It did not build cars again until 1959. Mitsubishi entered the U.S. market in 1971 — not as Mitsubishi but as the Dodge Colt. Chrysler Corp. still markets Mitsubishi cars in the United States, but so does Mitsubishi.

Why did Japan overtake and in many ways beat the United States at its own automotive game?

Many explanations have been offered. Management blames high labor costs in the United States, unions blame poor and greedy management. The unions gained credibility when Japanese makers began assembling cars in the United States and managed to obtain high levels of quality with American workers.

The first overseas maker in modern times to assemble cars in the United States was Volkswagen, German maker with a high reputation for quality, and it reported the same results — that quality achieved by American workers was on a par with that of its German plants.

Many observers blame American management's focus on short-term financial performance with the U.S. decline in the face of long-range Japanese investment in zero-defect quality and technological excellence. American managers, they say, are more interested in their salary and perquisites than in growth and investors are looking for the quick buck.

Craftsmen who put their names on their products and took personal interest in them built the American auto industry. They wanted to make money, of course, but this was secondary to their dreams of automotive glory.

Now craftsmen are out of style, working with the hands is held in contempt, company loyalty is discouraged, wisdom in the form of older workers is junked and next quarter's results are perhaps too important. The evidence is that the MBAs had a lot more to do with America's decline than the UAW.

Somewhere West of Laramie

SOMEWHERE west of Laramie there's a broncho-busting, steer-roping girl who knows what I'm talking about. She can tell what a sassy pony, that's a cross between greased lightning and the place where it hits, can do with eleven hundred pounds of steel and action when he's going high, wide and handsome.

The truth is—the Playboy was built for her.

Built for the lass whose face is brown with the sun when the day is done of revel and romp and race.

She loves the cross of the wild and the tame.

There's a savor of links about that car—of laughter and lilt and light—a hint of old loves—and saddle and quirt. It's a brawny thing—yet a graceful thing for the sweep o' the Avenue.

Step into the Playboy when the hour grows dull with things gone dead and stale.

Then start for the land of real living with the spirit of the lass who rides, lean and rangy, into the red horizon of a Wyoming twilight.

JORDAN

JORDAN MOTOR CAR COMPANY, Inc., Cleveland, Ohio

A legendary feat of copywriting (1923).

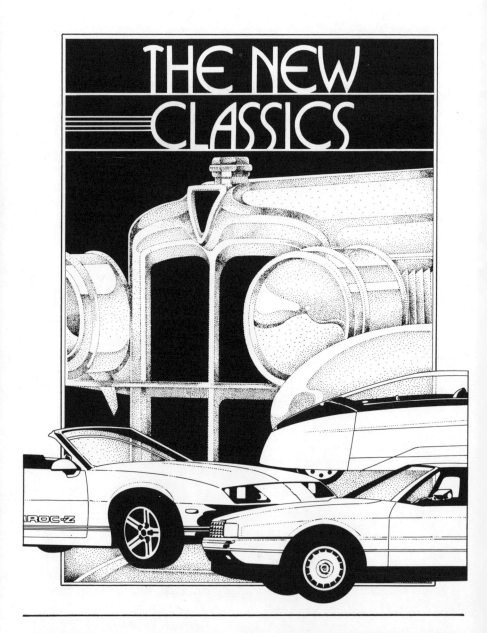

THE NEW
CLASSICS

Second century of auto is off to a rousing start

In this 101st year of the automobile, there was another stockholder revolt, this time at General Motors. It was only one stockholder who challenged management, but it was the biggest stockholder of all.

L. Ross Perot, founder and chairman of Electronic Data Systems Inc., became GM's largest single shareholder when GM acquired the computer firm in an effort to step immediately to the head of the high-tech line.

Unlike earlier stockholder rebels (and there have been plenty of them in the auto industry), Perot was not charging corruption, or stupidity, or insensitivity to vital issues. He was not even charging mismanagement. He was not really charging anything.

But what he had to say GM did not want to hear. He seemed to be saying that GM has lost its "can-do" vigor.

GM's Roger B. Smith said Perot meant nothing of the sort, that he didn't really know how to run a modern multinational giant like GM. So GM bought out Perot at a very good price and Perot agreed to shut up.

Many financial analysts agreed with Smith. Perot was a throwback, a character from an earlier, more romantic and more individualistic age, a man who masterminded a dramatic rescue of hostages in Iran, built a giant computer firm from nothing, aids Vietnam veterans and does other good works. In short, he was a man who would probably have felt right at home with the founders of the auto industry.

Smith might well have been right and may have been acting prudently to protect the corporation from a man who has achieved mythic status, but in fact had never built an automobile. But the confrontation, so out of character for GM, nonetheless raised issues and questions. And not only about GM. About the American auto industry. About Detroit.

Is GM no longer the "can-do" company that optimistically grew like Topsy in the early days of this century, that took on Ford's beloved Model T and beat it, that helped make Detroit the arsenal of democracy during World War II?

Was this the innovative organization that gave the world the electric self-starter (with a whole new battery-based ignition system to boot), that was the first and for a long time the only auto maker with an automatic transmission that worked well, that developed an engine of such efficiency that it would not run on available fuel and so developed a new fuel to run it?

How can General Motors, which built the Chevrolet that finally conquered Ford in the lower-price arena, say it can't build small cars in America, that it cannot build an entry-level car as good as the Japanese?

After so many decades of building one of the world's great luxury cars, after making Cadillac "the standard of the world" and suffering "the penalty of leadership", how did GM fall so far behind Mercedes-Benz, BMW, Volvo, Audi and Jaguar?

The Smith-Perot confrontation seems in retrospect to be about bureaucracy and complacency. Perot was not attacking Smith, he was attacking a mindset, an attitude. He struck a blow at complacency, but that complacency had probably been wiped out some time ago. There is evidence that Detroit is coming out of its dark age.

Great cars are spawned by hard times. It seems that good times lead to mediocrity, hard times to greatness.

Some of the greatest, most magnificent cars built in America or in Europe were built in the depths of the Great Depression.

The Depression was ended by World War II and we had pretty good times since the end of that war, until the first oil crisis hit in 1973-74. Detroit peaked in 1973. But that was also the depth of its dark age. It has been bedeviled since then, but has also made enormous advances. It has come a long way.

In 1973, sales of American-built cars hit 9.7 million units and total sales in the United States reached 11.4 million. Total sales have topped '73 since then, but not domestic. Times were never as good again for Detroit.

But that's the view from the sales department and from the financial department. From the engineering department, things look great.

And from the car buyer's vantage point, times have never been better. Those magnificent classics, those Duesenbergs and Bugattis that Tom Monaghan has stuffed in that barn out in Ann Arbor are wonderful, but the average car buyer has never had it so good. These are, indeed, the good old days.

The Duesenbergs, Cadillacs, Packards, Cords, Auburns and Stutzes of the early '30s were wonderful cars, but they were for the rich. Today's classics are more proletarian Fords, Chevrolets and Dodges. It may be hard to accept in this age when we seem to be losing ground to the Japanese, the Koreans, maybe even the Malaysians and the Yugoslavs, but the American car is moving back to greatness. This is the age of the new classics.

In the automobile world, "classic" has a specific meaning. It does not just mean an old car or a favorite car, says Dean Kruse, leading auctioneer of classic cars based in that '30s capital of classics, Auburn, Ind. It refers to a car that is special in some way, out of the ordinary.

The Classic Car Club of America lists particular models that are "classics." It says, for example, that all Duesenbergs, Cords, Mercers, Hispano-Suizas and Pierce-Arrows made between 1925 and 1948 are classics, while only certain specified models of Cadillac, Packard, Lincoln, Mercedes-Benz and Chrysler are and only custom-bodied Buicks and Hudsons.

Well, what about the '49 Ford or the '55 Chevy? What about the '53 Corvette or the '55 Thunderbird? What about the Studebaker Hawks or the GTO or Jaguar XKE? What about the Volkswagen Beetle? Many *aficianados* call cars such as these "classics" because they were cars that generated unusual and undying fondness.

Technically, they are not "classic cars," but in the popular use of the word they are "of the highest class," "having recognized worth."

In that sense of the word, more American "classics" are coming on the market to join the Volvos, Hondas, Mercedes-Benz, BMWs and Mazdas as modern classics for everyone.

Cars of excellent design and high-tech features, such as Ford's Thunderbird/Cougar and Taurus/Sable, are changing the concept of the American car.

Chrysler's new LeBaron Coupe and Chevrolet's Beretta and Corsica are challenging Ford's front-runners, once scorned as "jellybeans" and "flying potatos."

At the upper end, where the classics of the '30s were positioned, Detroit long ago left the field to such European marques as Rolls-Royce, Ferrari and Lamborghini. But now it appears interested again.

The Cadillac Allante and Chrysler Maserati may be the first tentative steps back toward the automotive peaks where excellence, not volume, is the goal. Those peaks were once held by American makes, but not since the hard, desperate days of the Great Depression.

Now times are hard again. Not in the sense that companies are in danger of going under (although this was the case just a few years ago). Now the times are hard on Detroit's battered pride, on its jobs which continue to languish while profits rebound and on its position as the Motor City, spiritual center of the auto world.

Selling cars made in Japan, Korea, Mexico and Brazil may result in profits for the American makers. But it is hardly a source of pride. And it will certainly not make it the pillar of the American economy that Detroit has traditionally been.

The '87 crop of cars is the best in history. Twenty years ago, car buff publications ran road tests which lauded the "good cars," that is, cars that performed well, handled well and had style and flair. They were the exception, now the rule.

Readers were warned about the big luxury cars with marshmallow suspension and living-room interiors that were not good road cars, were not safe.

Now the job of the auto magazines is different. It is to describe the ways in which the cars differ, their strong points and weak. But almost all are "good." Some are better than others, but design has come a long way in the last few years

There is no reason that Detroit should not once more take the heights. Its engineering and technology are still unmatched. Volkswagen and the Japanese have proved that American workers are as good as any anywhere. What it takes is the will to do it, the drive for excellence in automobiles rather than in the next quarter's balance sheet. Maybe that was what Perot had in mind.

There is reason to believe that Detroit's priorities are changing, that in desperate response to the international challenge it will resort once more to true automotive excellence, to the building of "classic cars."

Why not a four-valve-per-cylinder aluminum-block V-16 Cadillac or V-12 Lincoln or turbocharged Chrysler Imperial with distinctive styling, computer controls, four-wheel drive, anti-lock braking and all the other modern amenities and hang the expense?

So what if a car costs $100,000 and its volume is low? It would demonstrate that the goal is excellence and that's important. Excellence has a way of "trickling down."

Maybe more was read into that confrontation in the 101st year than should have been. Chrysler's bid to acquire AMC was almost an anti-climax. It was a big story, but there was no controversy. It was a big story because it was history. It tied things together neatly. Chrysler and Nash are back together again.

The second century is off to a rousing start.

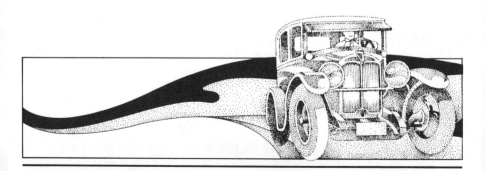

Grandpa's world gone, changed beyond recall

If you are now in middle age, the chance is good that your grandparents were born before the automobile worked its enormous change on American life. In about three generations electrical power, the telephone, radio, TV, airplanes, computers, even space travel, have changed the way we live beyond recognition. But no invention has changed our day-to-day life quite so much as the automobile.

Its change is so pervasive it is hard to grasp.

Many of the names of those earliest automotive pioneers are still around on car nameplates — Henry Ford, David Buick, Ransom E. Olds, Louis Chevrolet, John and Horace Dodge, Walter P. Chrysler here in the United States; Gottlieb Daimler, Karl Benz and Adam Opel in Germany; Armond Peugeot, Louis Renault and Andre Citroen in France and in Great Britain, C.S. Rolls and Henry Royce.

Many more have had their day of glory and passed on as the auto industry whittled down the thousands of makers who have entered the game into the highly concentrated world industry that exists today.

A lot has happened since Karl Benz got that first car working well enough to put it into production. But it has not really been a very long time.

Grandpa can remember when the world was a lot different.

THE TOP 40 OF WORLD MOTOR VEHICLE MANUFACTURERS

Motor vehicle makers of the world (with home country), listed in order of world-wide 1985 production. Data was gathered from various sources by the Motor Vehicle Manufacturers Assn., Detroit.

General Motors (U.S.) 9,077,049.
General Motors-U.S., 6,425,505.
GM-Canada, 843,449.
Opel, W. Germany, 938,071.
Vauxhall, UK, 213,370.
GM-Spain, 277,101.
GM-Brazil, 222,801.
GM-Mexico, 55,705.
GM-Holden, 101,047.

Ford Motor Co. (U.S.), 5,450,526
Ford-U.S., 2,852,577.
Ford-Canada, 657,116.
Ford-W. Germany, 505,231.
Ford-Belgium, 303,430.
Ford-UK, 419,096.
Ford Spain, 265,884.

Ford-Brazil, 189,073.
Ford-Mexico, 74,364.
Ford-Australia, 153,314.
Ford-Argentina, 29,441.

Toyota, (Japan), 3,718,522.
Toyota-Japan, 3,665,622.
Toyota-Australia, 50,315.
Toyota-Brazil, 2,585.

Nissan (Japan), 2,808,085.
Nissan-Japan, 2,536,439
Nissan-Mexico, 68,317.
Nissan-Australia, 44,225.
Nissan Iberica-Spain, 7,872.
Nissan-U.S.A., 151,232.

Volkswagen (Germany), 2,385,349.
  VW-W. Germany, 1,457,272.
  VW Audi-W. Germany, 358,612.
  VW-Argentina, 20,059.
  VW-Brazil, 357,696.
  VW-Mexico, 94,979.
  VW-U.S.A., 96,458.

Chrysler Corp. (U.S.), 1,936,583.
  Chrysler-U.S.A., 1,479,998.
  AMC/Eagle, 357,512.
  Chrysler-Canada, 390,120.
  Chrysler-Mexico, 66,465.

Renault Regie, (France), 1,879,054.
  Renault-France, 1,535,591.
  Renault-Alpine, 1,312.
  Renault-Argentina, 41,294.
  Renault-Mexico, 19,779.
  Renault FASA, Spain, 245,725.
  Renault RVI, Spain, 2,763.
  Renault RTI/Karrier, UK, 5,022.
  Mack, U.S.A., 24,279.
  Mack, Canada, 3,289.

Peugeot S.A., (France), 1,818,816.
  Peugeot-France, 895,812.
  Citroen-France, 553,119.
  Talbot-France, 30,027.
  Sevel Peugeot, Italy, 36,781.
  Talbot-Spain, 95,850.
  Citroen-Spain, 140,161.
  Talbot-UK, 67,066.

UAZ (U.S.S.R), 1,660,000.
  Lada, 785,000.
  Vans, 875,000.

Fiat (Italy), 1,508,986.
  Fiat-Italy, 993,923.
  Lancia-Italy, 127,322.

Autobianchi-Italy, 99,896.
Iveco-Italy, 82,846.
Sevel Fiat-Italy, 39,277.
Ferrari, 3,125.
Fiat-Argentina, 806.
Fiat-Brazil, 151,111.
Unic, France, 99.
Iveco-Magirus-Germany, 10,581.

Honda (Japan), 1,265,648.
  Honda-Japan, 1,120,311.
  Honda-U.S., 145,337.

Mazda (Japan), 1,193,692.

Mitsubishi (Japan), 1,152,777.

Suzuki (Japan), 781,901.

Daimler-Benz (Germany) 741,138.
  Mercedes-Benz-W.Germany, 669,188.
  Mercedes-Benz-Argentina, 3,344.
  Mercedes-Benz-Brazil, 33,013.
  Mercedes-Benz-Spain, 10,910.
  Mercedes-Benz-U.S., 4,516.
  Freightliner, U.S., 17,709.
  Freightliner, Canada, 2,458.

Isuzu (Japan), 587,015.

Fuji (Japan), 584,384.

Daihatsu (Japan), 578,937.

BL (United Kingdom), 577,060.
  Austin Rover-UK, 496,150.
  Layland Vehicles-UK, 59,398.
  Santana Land-Rover-Spain, 21,512.

Volvo (Sweden), 456,959.
  Volvo-Sweden, 323,648.
  Volvo BV-Holland, 108,328.

Volvo-Brazil, 3,559.
Volvo-Canada, 10,078.
Volvo-UK, 26.
Volvo-U.S., 11,320.

BMW (W. Germany), 431,085.

SEAT (Spain), 320,015.

Polski Fiat (Poland), 259,245.

Hyundai (South Korea), 240,755.

Skoda (Czechoslovakia), 226,342.

Moskvitch (U.S.S.R.), 200,000.

Zastava (Yugoslavia), 166,618.

Alfa Romeo (Italy), 160,563.

ZAZ Zaporozhets (USSR), 150,000.

Saab-Scania (Sweden), 142,662.
Saab-Sweden, 111,813.
Scania-Sweden, 25,611.

Scania-Argentina, 865.
Scania-Brazil, 4,373.

Trabant (E. Germany), 141,795.

GAZ Volga (U.S.S.R.), 127,000.

Jaefang (China), 85,003.

Kia (South Korea), 84,931.

Navistar (U.S.), 84,931.
Navistar-U.S., 71,925.
Navistar-Canada, 10,702.
Seddon Atkinson-UK, 1,667.

Wartburg (E. Germany), 84,000.

Aeolus (China), 83,431.

Hino (Japan), 69,063.

Porsche (West Germany), 54,431.

Daewoo (South Korea), 44,935.

MAJOR NAMEPLATES PRODUCED THROUGHOUT THE WORLD IN THE FIRST 101 YEARS.

AUSTRALIA
Ford, 1925-present, Campbellfield, Victoria.
Harnett, 1951-57, Melbourne.
Holden, 1948-present, Melbourne.
Tarrant, 1901-07, Melbourne.

AUSTRIA
Austro-Daimler, 1899-1936, Wiener-Neustadt.
Austro-Fiat, 1921-36, Vienna.
Lohner, 1896-1906, Vienna.
Nesselsdorf, 1897-1920, Nesselsdorf.
Puch, 1906-25, Graz.
Steyr, 1920-40; 1953-76, Steyr; Graz.
W.A.F., 1910-26, Vienna.

BELGIUM
Dasse, 1894-1924, Verviers.
DeChamps, 1899-1906, Brussels.
Excelsior, 1903-32, Brussels; Saventhem; Nessonvaux-les-Liege.

BELGIUM
Dasse, 1894-1924, Verviers.
DeChamps, 1899-1906, Brussels.
Excelsior, 1903-32, Brussels; Saventhem; Nessonvaux-les-Liege.
Germain, 1897-1914, Monceau-sur-Sambre
Imperia, 1906-49, Nessonvaux.
Metallurgique, 1898-1928, Marchienne-au-Pont.
Miesse, 1896-1926, Brussels.
Minerva, 1899-1939, Antwerp.
Nagant, 1900-28, Liege.
Pipe, 1898-1922, Brussels.
Vivinus, 1899-1912, Brussels.

CANADA
Frontenac, 1931-33, Leaside, Ont.
Galt, 1911-13, Galt, Ont.
LeRoy, 1899-1907, Kitchener, Ont.
Maritime Six, 1913-14, St. John, N.B.
McLaughlin, 1908-22, Oshawa, Ont.
McLaughlin-Buick, 1923-42, Oshawa.
Regal, 1914-17, Kitchener, Ont.
Tudhope, 1908-13, Orillia, Ont.

CHINA
Beijing, 1958-present, Beijing.
Hong Qi, 1953-present, Dongfeng Dajie.
Shanghai, 1959-present, Shanghai.

CZECHOSLOVAKIA
Praga, 1907-47, Prague.
Skoda, 1923-present, Pilsen; Mlada Boleslav.
Tatra, 1923-present, Koprivnice.
Wikov, 1929-36, Prostejov.

FRANCE
Alcyon, 1906-28, Courbevoie.
Alpine, 1955-present, Dieppe.
Amilcar, 1921-39, St Denis; Boulogne-sur-Seine.
Berliot, 1895-1939, Lyons.
Bignan, 1918-30, Courbevoie.
Brasier, 1897-30, Ivry-port.
Buc, Buccial, 1923-33, Courbevoie.
Buchet, 1911-29, Levallois-Perret.
Bugatti, 1909-1956, Molsheim.
C.G.V., Charron, 1901-30, Puteaux.
Chenard-Walcker, 1901-46, Asnieres, Gennevilliers.
Citroen, 1919-present, Paris.
Clement, Clement-Bayard, 1899-1922, Levallois-Perret, Mezieres.

Packard-like Russian ZIS limousine went out with Stalin;
below, the '57 Czech Tatra was highly innovative

Corre; La Licorne, 1901-50, Courbevoie.
Cottereau, 1898-1910, Dijon.
Cottin-Desgouttes, 1905-33, Lyons.
Darracq, 1896-1959, Suresnes.
D.B., 1938-61, Champigny-sur-Marne
De Bazelaire, 1907-28, Paris.
Decauville, 1898-1910, Corbeil.
De Dietrich, 1897-1934, Luneville, Argenteuil.
De Dion-Bouton, 1883-1932, Paris, Puteaux.
Delage, 1905-54, Courbevoie, Paris.
Delahaye, 1894-1954, Paris.
Delaugere, 1901-26, Orleans.
Delaunay-Belleville, 1904-50, St Denis.
D.F.P., 11906-26, Courbevoie.
Facel-Vega, 1954-64, Pont-a-Mousson.
Gauthier, 1904-37, La Garenne-Colombes; Blois.
Georges Irat, 1921-46, Chatou; Neuilly; Levallois-Perret.
Georges Roy, 1906-29, Bordeaux.
Gladiator, 1896-20, Pre-St Gervais; Puteaux.
Gobron-Brillie, 1898-1918, Boulogne-sur-Seine.
Gobron, 1919-30, Lavallois-Perret.
Gordini, 1951-57, Paris.
Hispano-Suiza, 1911-38, Lavallois-Perret; Bois-Colombes.
Hotchkiss, 1903-55, St Denis.
Hurtu, 1896-1930, Albert; Neuilly; Rueil.
Krieger, 1897-1909, Paris; Colombes,
La Buire, 1904-30, Lyons.
Lacoste et Battmann, 1897-1913, Paris.
Lambert, 1926-53, Macon; Reims; Giromagny.
Leon Bolle; Morris-Leon Bollee, 1895-1933, Le Mans.
Leon Laisne; Harris-Leon Laisne;

Harris, 1920-37, Lille; Nantes.
LeZebre, 1909-32, Puteaux.
Mass, 1903-23, Courbevoie.
Mathis, 1898-1950, Strasbourg.
Matra, 1965, Romorantin; Velizy-Villacoublay.
Pierron, 1912-23, Courbevoie.
Mieusset, 1903-14, Lyons.
Mors, 1895-25; 1941-43, Paris.
Omega, 1922-30, Boulogne-sur-Seine.
Panhard, 1889-1967, Paris.
Passe-Partout, 1901-30, Neuilly, Levallois-Perret.
Peugeot, 1889-present, Beaulieu-Valentigney; Audincourt; Sochaux.
Pilain, 1902-20, Lyons.
Renault, 1898-present, Billancourt; Flins; Havre-Sandouville.
Rochet-Schneider, 1894-1932, Lyons.
Rolland-Pilain, 1906-31, Tours.
Rosengart, 1928-55, Neuilly-sur-Seine; Paris.
Rossel, 1903-26, Sochaux-Mont-beliard.
Salmson, 1921-57, Billancourt.
Serpollet, 1887-1907, Paris.
Simca, 1935-80, Nanterre; Poissy.
Tracta, 1926-34, Asnieres.
Turcat-Mery, 1898-1928, Marseilles.
Unic, 1904-39, Puteaux.
Vespa, 1958-61, Fourchamboult.
Vinot, 1901-26, Puteaux; Nanterre.
Voisin, 1919-39, Issy-les- Moulineaux.

GERMANY
Adler, 1900-39, Frankfurt.
Amphicar, 1961-68, Lubeck-Schlutup
Audi, 1910-present, Zwickau; Ingolstadt.
Auto Union, 1958-62, Dusseldorf, Ingolstadt.

Benz, 1886-26, Mannheim.
Benz Sohne, 1906-26, Ladenburg/Neckar.
BMW, 1928-present, Munich.
Borgward, 1939-61, Bremen.
Brennabor, 1908-1934, Brandenburg.
Daimler, 1886-1902, Bad Cannstatt.
D.K.W., 1928-66, Berlin; Dusseldorf; Ingolstadt.
Durkopp, 1898-1927.
E.M.W., 1945-55, Eisenach
Ford, 1931-present, Cologne.
Framo, 1932-37, Frankenberg; Hainichen.
Goliath, 1931-63, Bremen.
Hanomag, 1924-39, Hanover.
Hansa, 1906-39, Bielefeld; Bremen.
Hansa-Lloyd, 1921-29, Bremen.
Horch, 1900-39, Cologne; Zwickau.
Lloyd, 1906-14; 1950-63, Bremen.
Maico, 1955-58, Pfaffingen; Herrenberg.
Maybach, 1921-41, Friedrichshafen.
Mercedes, 1901-26, Bad Cannstatt; Stuttgart.
Mercedes-Benz, 1926-present, Stuttgart, Mannheim.
Messerschmitt, 1953-62, Regensburg.
N.A.G., 1902-34, Berlin.
N.S.U., 1905-80, Neckarsulm.
Opel, 1898-present, Russelsheim.
Oryx, 1907-22, Berlin.
Piccolo, 1904-12, Apolda.
Porsche, 1948-present, Gmund (Austria); Stuttgart.
Protos, 1900-26, Berlin.
Rohr, 1928-35, Ober-Ramstadt.
Stoewer, 1899-1939, Stettin.
Trabant, 1959-present, Zwickau.
Volkswagen, 1936-present, Stuttgart; Berlin; Wolfsburg.
Wanderer, 1911-39, Schonau; Siegmar.

Wartburg, 1898-1904, Eisenach.
Wartburg, 1956-present, Eisenach.

ITALY
Abarth, 1950-71, Torino.
Alfa Romeo, 1910-present, Milan, Naples.
Bianchi, 1899-1939, Milan.
Ceirano, 1919-31, Torino.
Chiribiri, 1913-27, Torino.
Cistalia, 1946-65, Torino,
De Tomaso, 1959-present, Modena.
Diatto, 1905-27, Torino.
Ferrari, 1940-present, Modena.
Fiat, 1899-present, Torino.
Innocenti, 1961-present, Milan.
Intermeccanica, 1967-present, Torino.
Isetta, 1953-55, Milan.
Isotta-Fraschini, 1900-49, Milan.
Itala, 1904-34, Torino.
Lamborghini, 1963-present, Agata Bolognese.
Lancia, 1906-present, Torino.
Maserati, 1926-present, Bologna; Modena.
Nazzaro, 1911-23, Torino; Florence.
O.M., 1918-34, Brescia.
Osca, 1947-67, Bologna.
Rapid, 1906-21, Torino.
Siata, 1949-70, Torino.

JAPAN
Chiyoda, 1932-35, Tokyo.
Daihatsu, 1954-present, Osaka.
Dat, Datson, Datsun, 1912-present, Tokyo, Osaka, Yokohama.
Hino, 1953-67, Tokyo.
Honda, 1962-present, Tokyo.
Isuzu, 1953-present, Tokyo.
Mazda, 1960-present, Hiroshima.

Mitsubishi, 1917-21; 1959- present, Kobe; Tokyo.
Nissan, 1937-43; 1960-present, Yokohama.
Ohta, 1922; 1934-57, Tokyo.
Prince, 1952-67, Tachikawa; Tokyo.
Subaru, 1958-present, Tokyo.
Sumida, 1933-37, Tokyo.
Suzuki, 1961-present, Hamamatsu.
Toyota, 1936-present, Kariya; Tokyo.

NETHERLANDS
DAF, 1958-present, Endhoven.
Eysin, 1899-1920, Amersfoort.
Spijker, 1900-25, Amsterdam.

POLAND
Polski Fiat, 1968-present, Warsaw.
Syrena, 1955-72, Warsaw.
Warszawa, 1951-72, Warsaw.

SOVIET UNION
Chaika, 1958-present, Gorky.
Lada, 1969-present, Togliatti.
Moskvitch, 1947-present, Moscow.
Pobieda, 1946-58, Gorky.
Volga, 1955-present, Gorky.
Zaporozhets, 1960-present, Moscow.
ZIL, 1947-present, Moscow.

SPAIN
Hispano-Suiza, 1904-44, Barcelona.
Nacional Pescara, 1929-32, Barcelona.
Pegaso, 1951-58, Barcelona.
SEAT, 1953-present, Barcelona.

SWEDEN
Saab, 1950-present, Linkoping.
Scania, 1902-12, Malmo.
Scania-Vabis, 1914-29, Sodertalje.
Volvo, 1927-present, Gothenburg.

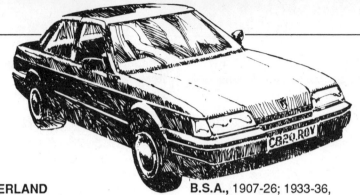

SWITZERLAND
Martini, 1897-1934, Frauenfeld; St
Blaise-Neuchatel.
Moser, 1914-24, St Aubin.
Pic-Pic, 1906-24, Geneva.
Saurer, 1897-1914, Arbon.
Sbarro, 1971-present, Gressy.
Stella, 1906-13, Geneva.
Turicum, 1904-14, Zurich.

UNITED KINGDOM
A.C., 1908-73, London; Surrey.
Allard, 1937-60, London.
Alvis, 1920-67, Coventry.
Argyll, 1899-1932, Glasgow.
Armstrong Siddeley, 1919-60,
Coventry.
Arrol-Aster, 1897-1931, Glasgow;
Heathhall.
Arrol-Johnston, 1897-1931,
Glasgow; Heathhall.
Aston Martin, 1922-present, London,
Feltham, Newport Pagnell.
Austin, 1906-present, Longbridge,
Birmingham.
Austin-Healey, 1953-71, Longbridge;
Abingdon.
Bean, 1919-29, Dudley.
Belsize, 1897-1925, Manchester.
Bentley, 1920-present, London; Derby;
Crewe.
Bond, 1949-70, Preston.
Bristol, 1947-present, Filton, Bristol.

B.S.A., 1907-26; 1933-36,
Sparkbrook; Coventry.
B.S.A., 1929-40, Birmingham.
Buckingham, 1913-23, Coventry.
Calthorpe. 1904-32, Birmingham.
Chambers, 1904-25, Belfast.
Clyde, 1901-30, Leicester.
Clyno, 1922-30, Wolverhampton;
Birmingham.
Connaught, 1949-57, Surrey.
Cooper, 1948-69, Surrey.
Crossley, 1904-37, Manchester.
Daimler, 1896-present, Coventry.
Elva, 1955-68, Sussex; Croyden;
Shenley.
Fergus, 1915-21, Belfast.
Ford, 1911-present, Manchester;
Dagenham.
Frazer Nash, 1924-60, Isleworth.
Hampton, 1911-33, Hampton- in-Arden;
King's Norton; Stroud.
Hillman, 1907-78, Coventry; Ryton-on-
Dunsmore; Glasgow.
Horstmann, 1914-29, Bath.
Humber, 1898-75, Beeston; Coventry;
Ryton-on-Dunsmore.
Invicta, 1925-38; 1946-50, Surrey;
London.
Jaguar, 1945-present, Coventry.
Jensen, 1936-75, West Bromwich.
Jewel, 1921-39, Bradford.
Jowett, 1906-54, Bradford.
Lagonda, 1906-63, Staines; Feltham,
Newport Pagnell.

Lanchester, 1895-1956, Birmingham.
Lea-Francis, 1904-06; 1920-35; 1937-53; 1960, Coventry.
Leyland, 1920-23, Leyland.
Lloyd, 1936-51, Grimsby.
Lotus, 1952-present, London; Cheshunt; Norwich.
Maudslay, 1902-23, Coventry.
McLaren, 1964-present, Slough; Rye; Croyden.
MG, 1924-present, Oxford; Abingdon.
Morgan, 1910-present, Malvern Link.
Morris, 1913-present, Crowley.
Napier, 1900-24, London.
Ogle, 1961-64, Letchworth.
Owen, 1899-1935, London.
Palladium, 1912-25, London.
Pennington, 1896-99, Coventry; London.
Phoenix, 1903-28, London; Letchworth.
Rapier, 1933-40, Staines; London.
Reliant, 1952-present, Tamworth.
Rex, 1901-14, Birmingham; Coven- try.
Riley, 1898-1969, Coventry; Abingdon.
Rolls-Royce, 1904-present, Manchester; Derby; Crewe.
Rover, 1904-present, Coventry; Birmingham; Solihull.
Scout, 1904-23, Salisbury; Pewsey.
Singer, 1905-70, Coventry; Ryton-on-Dunsmore.
S.S., 1931-45, Coventry.
Standard, 1903-63, Coventry.
Stanhope, 1915-25, Leeds.
Star, 1898-1932, Wolverhampton.
Storey, 1919-30, London.
Straker-Squire, 1906-26, Bristol; London.
Sunbeam, 1899-1937; 1953-78, Wolverhampton, London, Ryton-on-Dunsmore.

Sunbeam-Talbot, 1938-54, London, Ryton-on-Dunsmore.
Swift, 1900-31, Coventry.
Talbot, 1903-38, London.
Thornycroft, 1903-13, Basingstoke.
Triumph, 1923-present, Coventry.
Trojan, 1922-36; 1961-65, Kingston-on-Thames; Croyden.
Turner, 1906-07; 1911-30, Wolverhampton,
TVR, 1954-present, Blackpool.
Vanden Plas, 1960-70, London.
Vauxhall, 1903-present, London; Luton.
Vulcan, 1902-28, Southport.
Waverley, 1910-31, London.
Whitlock, 1903-32, London.
Wolseley, 1899-1974, Birmingham; Cowley.

UNITED STATES

Abbott, 1909-18, Detroit; Cleveland.
A.B.C., 1906-10, St. Louis.
Ace, 1920-22, Ypsilanti, Mich.
Acme, 1903-10, Reading, Pa.
Adams-Farwell, 1904-13, Dubuque.
Aerocar, 1906-08, Detroit.
Airphibian, 1950-56, Danbury, Conn.
Ajax, 1901-03, New York.
Ajax, 1914-15, Seattle, Wash.
Ajax, 1925-26, Racine, Wis.
Aland, 1916-17, Detroit.
Alco, 1905-13, Providence, R.I.
Allen, 1914-22, Columbus; Bucyrus; Fostoria, Ohio.
Alliance, 1984-87, Kenosha, Wis.
Allstate, 1952-53, Willow Run, Mich.
All-Steel, 1915-16, St. Louis.
Alpena Flyer, 1910-14, Alpena, Mich.
Alter, 1914-17, Grand Haven, Mich.
Ambassador (Yellow Cab), 1922-26, Chicago.

American, 1916-20, Lafayette, Ind.
American, 1916-24, Plainfield, N.J.
American Austin, 1930-34, Butler, Pa.
American Bantam, 1934-41, Butler, Pa.
American Electric, 1899-1902, Chicago; Hoboken, N.J.
American Mercedes, 1904-07, Long Island, N.Y.
American Motors, 1968-present, Detroit; Southfield, Mich.
American Simplex, 1906-10, Mishawaka, Ind.
American Steam Car, 1929-31, West Newton, Mass.
American Steamer, 1922-24, Chicago, Elgin, Ill.
American Underslung, 1906-14, Indianapolis.
American Voiturette, 1913, Detroit.
Ames, 1910-15, Owensboro, Ky.
Amplex, 1910-15, Mishawaka, Ind.
Anderson, 1916-26, Rock Hill, S.C.
Anhut, 1909-10, Detroit.
Ann Arbor, 1911-12, Ann Arbor.
Apollo, 1962-64, Oakland, Pasadena, Calif.
Apperson, 1902-26, Kokomo, Ind.

Apple, 1917-18, Dayton, Ohio.
ArBenz, 1911-18, Chillicothe, Ohio.
Argo, 1912-14, Saginaw, Mich.
Argo, 1914-16, Jackson, Mich.
Arnolt, 1953-63, Chicago.
Asheville, 1914-15, Asheville, N.C.
Atlas, 1907-11, Springfield, Mass.
Atlas-Knight, 1911-13, Springfield, Mass.
Auburn, 1900-37, Auburn, Ind.
Aurora, 1906-08, Aurora, Ill.
Austin, 1901-21, Grand Rapids, Mich.
Auto-Bug, 1909-10, Norwalk, Ohio.
Autocar, 1897-1911, Pittsburgh; Ardmore, Pa.
Autoette, 1910-13, Manistee, Mich.
Automotor, 1901-04, Springfield, Mass.
Avanti, 1962-64, South Bend, Ind.
Avanti II, 1965-present, South Bend, Ind.
Babcock Electric, 1906-12, Buffalo.
Badger, 1909-12, Clintonville, Wis.
Baker Electric, 1899-1916, Cleveland.
Balzer, 1894-1900, New York City.
Barley, 1922-24, Kalamazoo, Mich.
Barnes, 1910-12, Sandusky, Ohio.
Bates, 1903-05, Lansing, Mich.

Beggs, 1918-23, Kansas City, Mo.
Beisel, 1914, Monroe, Mich.
Bendix, 1907-10, Chicago; Logansport, Ind.
Berkshire, 1905-13, Pittsfield, Cambridge, Mass.
Berwick, 1904, Grand Rapids, Mich.
Biddle, 1915-23, Philadelphia.
Birch, 1917-23, Chicago.
Blomstrom, 1907-09, Detroit.
Blood, 1903-05, Kalamazoo, Mich.
Borland-Grannis, 1903-16, Chicago; Saginaw, Mich.
Boss, 1903-07, Reading, Pa.
Brewster, 1915-25, Long Island City, New York, N.Y.
Brewster, 1934-36, Springfield, Mass.
Briscoe, 1914-21, Jackson, Mich.
Brush, 1907-13, Detroit.
Buffalo, 1912-15, Buffalo, N.Y.
Buffum, 1901-07, Abington, Mass.
Buick, 1903-present, Flint, Mich.
Bush, 1916-24, Chicago.
Cadillac, 1903-present, Detroit.
Cameron, 1902-21, Pawtucket, R.I.; New London, West Haven, New Haven, Norwalk and Stamford, Conn.
Cannon, 1902-06, Kalamazoo.
Car De Luxe, 1906-10, Detroit, Toledo.
Carhartt, 1910-11, Detroit.
Carnation, 1912-14, Detroit.
Carroll, 1912-20, Strasburg, Pa.
Cartercar, 1906-16, Pontiac, Mich.
Case, 1910-27, Racine, Wis.
Century Electric, 1911-15, Detroit.
Chadwick, 1904-16, Chester, Philadelphia and Pottstown, Pa.
Chalmers, 1908-24, Detroit.
Chandler, 1913-29, Cleveland.
Chase, 1907-12, Syracuse, N.Y.

Checker, 1959-81, Kalamazoo, Mich.
Chevrolet, 1911-present, Detroit; Warren, Mich.
Chicago Steamer, 1905-07, Chicago.
Chicago Electric, 1915-16, Chicago.
Christie, 1904-10, New York; Hoboken, N.J.
Chrysler, 1923-present, Detroit; Highland Park, Mich.
Clark, 1900-09, Dorchester, Mass.
Clark, 1910-12, Lansing, Mich.
Clarkmobile, 1903-06, Lansing, Mich.
Cleveland, 1899-1901, Cleveland.
Cleveland, 1904-09, Cleveland.
Cleveland, 1919-26, Cleveland.
Climber, 1919-23, Little Rock, Ark.
Coey, 1913-17, Chicago.
Colburn, 1906-11, Denver.
Colby, 1911-14, Mason City, Iowa.
Cole, 1909-25, Indianapolis.
Columbia, 1897-1913, Hartford, Conn.
Columbia, 1916-24, Detroit.
Columbian, 1914-18, Detroit.
Columbus, 1903-13, Columbus, Ohio.
Cosmopolitan, 1907-10, St. Louis.
Crane, 1912-15, Bayonne and New Brunswick, N.J.
Crane-Simplex, 1915-24, New Brunswick, N.J.; Long Island City, N.Y.
Crawford, 1905-23, Hagerstown, N.J.
Crosley, 1939-52, Richmond and Marion, Ind.
Crow-Elkhart, 1909-24.
Croxton, 1911-14, Massilon and Cleveland, Ohio; Washington, Pa.
Croxton-Keeton, 1909-10, Massilon, Ohio.
Cunningham, 1907-36, Rochester, N.Y.
Cunningham, 1951-55, West Palm Beach, Fla.
Cutting, 1909-12, Jackson, Mich.
C.V.I., 1907-08, Jackson, Mich.

D.A.C., 1922-23, Detroit.
Dagmar, 1922-27, Hagerstown, Md.
Dalton, 1911-12, Flint, Mich.
Daniels, 1915-24, Reading, Philadelphia, Pa.
Davis, 1908-30, Baltimore.
Davis, 1947-49, Van Nuys, Calif.
Day Utility, 1922-24, Detroit.
Deal, 1905-11, Jonesville, Mich.
Demot, 1909-11, Detroit.
De Soto, 1913-16, Auburn, Ind.
De Soto, 1928-60, Detroit; Highland Park, Mich.
Detroit, 1899-02, Detroit.

Detroit, 1904-08, Detroit; Romeo, Mich.
Detroit-Dearborn, 1910-11, Dearborn, Mich.
Detroit Electric, 1907-38, Detroit.
Detroiter, 1912-17, Detroit.
Detroit-Oxford, 1905-06, Oxford, Mich.
Detroit Steam Car, 1922-23, Detroit.
Diamond T, 1905-11, Chicago.
Diana, 1925-28, St. Louis.
Dispatch, 1911-22, Minneapolis.
Dixie Flyer, 1916-23, Vincennes, Ind.; Louisville, Ky.

Doble, 1914-31, Waltham, Mass.;
Detroit; Emeryville, Calif.
Dodge Brothers, 1914-28, Detroit,
Hamtramck, Mich.
Dodge, 1928-present, Detroit;
Hamtramck, Highland Park. Mich.
Dolson, 1904-07, Charlotte, Mich.
Dorris, 1905-26, St. Louis.
Dort, 1915-24, Flint, Mich.
Duesenberg, 1920-37, Indianapolis.
Du Pont, 1920-32, Wilmington, Del.;
Moore, Pa.
Durant, 1921-32, New York; Lansing,
Mich.; Muncie, Ind.
Duryea, 1895-1913, Springfield,
Mass.; Peoria, Ill.; Reading, Pa.;
Saginaw, Mich.
Eagle, 1923-24, New York.
Eagle-Macomber, 1914-18, Sandusky,
Ohio.
Earl. 1921-23, Jackson, Mich.
Edsel, 1957-59, Dearborn, Mich.
Elcar, 1915-31, Elkhart, Ind.
Elgin, 1916-25, Argo, Ill.; Chicago.
Elkhart, 1908-09, Elkhart, Ind.
Elmore, 1900-12, Clyde, Ohio.
E.M.F., 1908-12, Detroit.
Empire, 1909-19, Indianapolis;
Greenville, Pa.
Enger, 1909-17, Cincinnati.
Erskine, 1926-30, South Bend, Ind.
Essex, 1918-32, Detroit.
Everitt, 1909-12, Detroit.
Excalibur, 1964-present, Milwaukee.
Falcon-Knight, 1927-28, Detroit.
Fiat, 1910-18, Poughkeepsie, N.Y.
Firestone-Columbus, 1907-15,
Columbus, Ohio.
Flanders, 1909-12, Detroit.
Flanders Electric, 1912-15, Pontiac;
Detroit.
Flint, 1902-04, Flint, Mich.

Flint, 1923-27, Long Island City, N.Y.;
Elizabeth, N.J., Flint, Mich.
Ford, 1903-present, Detroit; Dearborn,
Mich.
Franklin, 1901-34, Syracuse, N.Y.
Frazer, 1946-51, Willow Run, Mich.
Gardner, 1919-31, St. Louis.
Geronimo, 1917-20, Enid, Okla.
Graham-Paige, Graham, 1927-41,
Detroit.
Hackett, 1916-19, Jackson, Mich.
Hamlin-Holmes, 1919-30, Chicago;
Harvey, Ill.
Harroun, 1917-22, Wayne, Mich.
Haynes, 1904-25, Kokomo, Ind.
Haynes-Apperson, 1898-1904,
Kokomo.
Hertz, 1925-28, Chicago.
Hewitt, 1906-07, New York.
Honda, 1983-present, Marysville, Ohio.
Hudson, 1909-57, Detroit; Kenosha,
Wis.
Hupmobile, 1908-40, Detroit;
Cleveland.
Hupp-Yeats, 1911-19, Detroit.
Imperial, 1954-83, Detroit.
International, 1907-11, Chicago;
Akron, Ohio.
Inter-State, 1909-18, Muncie, Ind.
Jackson, 1903-23, Jackson, Mich.
Jeep, 1963-present, Toledo, Ohio.
Jeffery, 1914-17, Kenosha, Wis.
Jewett, 1923-26, Detroit.
Jordan, 1916-31, Cleveland.
Kaiser, 1946-54, Willow Run, Mich.
Kenworthy, 1920-22, Mishawaka, Ind.
King, 1910-24, Detroit; Buffalo.
King Midget, 1946-69, Athens, Ohio.
Kissel, 1906-31, Hartford, Wis.
Knox, 1900-15, Springfield, Mass.
Lafayette, 1920-24, Mars Hill, Ind.;
Milwaukee.

La Salle, 1927-40, Detroit.
Laurel, 1916-20, Anderson, Ind.
Lexington, 1909-28, Lexington, Ky.;
Connersville, Ind.
Liberty, 1916-24, Detroit.
Lincoln, 1920-present, Detroit;
Dearborn.
Little, 1912-15, Flint, Mich.
Locomobile, 1899-1929, Westboro,
Mass.; Bridgeport, Conn.
Lozier, 1905-17, Plattsburg, N.Y.;
Detroit.
Marion, 1904-15, Indianapolis.
Marion-Handley, 1916-19, Jackson,
Mich.
Marmon, 1902-33, Indianapolis.
Marquette, 1929-31, Flint, Mich.
Maxwell-Briscoe; Maxwell,
1904-25, Tarrytown, N.J.; Detroit.
Maytag, 1910-11, Waterloo, Iowa.
McFarlan, 1910-28, Connersville, Ind.
Mercer, 1910-25; 1931, Trenton, N.J.;
Elkhart, Ind.
Mercury, 1938-present, Dearborn,
Mich.
Metropolitan, 1954-61, Kenosha, Wis.
Milburn, 1914-22, Toledo.
Mitchell, 1903-23, Racine, Wis.
Moline; Moline-Knight, 1904- 29, E.
Moline, Ill.
Monroe, 1914-24, Flint, Pontiac, Mich.;
Indianapolis.
Moon, 1905-30, St. Louis.
Morriss-London, 1919-25, Elkhart,
Ind.
Muntz, 1949-54, Glendale, Calif.
Nash, 1917-57, Kenosha, Wis.
National, 1900-24, Indianapolis.
Nissan, 1985-present, Smyrna, Tenn.
Northern, 1902-09, Detroit.
Norwalk, 1910-22, Norwalk, Ohio;
Martinsburg, W. Va.

Oakland, 1907-31, Pontiac, Mich.
Ohio, 1909-13, Cincinnati.
Ohio, 1910-18, Toledo, Ohio.
Oldsmobile, 1896-present, Detroit;
Lansing, Mich.
O-We-Go, 1914-15, Owego, N.Y.
Owen, 1910-14, Detroit.
Owen Magnetic; Crown Magnetic,
1914-22, Wilkes-Barre, Pa.
Packard, 1899-1958, Warren, Ohio;
Detroit.
Paige-Detroit, 1908-27, Detroit.
Paterson, 1908-23, Flint, Mich.
Pathfinder, 1911-18, Indianapolis.
Peerless, 1900-31, Cleveland.
Pennington, 1896; 1899-1902,
Cleveland; Philadelphia.
Pierce; Pierce-Arrow, 1901-38,
Buffalo, N.Y.
Plymouth, 1928-present, Detroit.
Pontiac, 1926-present, Pontiac, Mich.
Pope-Hartford, 1903-14, Hartford,
Conn.
Pope-Toledo, 1903-09, Toledo, Ohio.
Pratt-Elkhart; Pratt, 1911-17,
Elkhart, Ind.
Premier, 1903-25, Indianapolis.
Pullman, 1903-17, York, Pa.
Pungs-Finch, 1904-10, Detroit.
Rainer, 1905-11, Saginaw, Mich.
Rambler, 1903-13; 1950-70, Kenosha,
Wis.
Rauch & Lang; Raulang, 1905-28,
Cleveland; Chickopee Falls, Mass.
Regal, 1907-20, Detroit.
Renault, 1981-87, Kenosha, Wis.
Reo, 1904-36, Lansing, Mich.
Richard, 1914-17, Cleveland.
Richmond, 1908-17, Richmond, Ind.
Rickenbacker, 1922-27, Detroit.
Roamer, 1916-30, Streator, Ill.;
Kalamazoo, Mich.

Rockne, 1931-33, Detroit.
Rolls-Royce, 1921-31, Springfield, Mass.
Roosevelt, 1929-31, Indianapolis.
Royal Tourist, 1904-11, Cleveland.
Ruxton, 1929-31, St. Louis; Milwaukee.
St Louis, 1898-1907, St. Louis; Peoria, Ill.
Saxon, 1913-23, Detroit; Ypsilanti, Mich.
Scarab, 1934-39, Detroit.
Schach, 1905-13, Cincinnati.
Scripps-Booth, 1913-22, Detroit.
Selden, 1906-14, Rochester, N.Y.
Senator, 1906-10, Ridgeville, Ind.
Seneca, 1917-24, Fostoria, Ohio.
Simplex, 1907-17, New Brunswick, N.J.
Smith; Great Smith, 1898-1911, Topeka, Kans.
Smith Flyer, 1917-19, Milwaukee.
Standard, 1912-23, Butler, Pa.
Stanley, 1897-1927, Newton, Mass.; Lawrence, Mass.

Star, 1922-28, Elizabeth, N.J.; Lansing, Mich.; Oakland, Calif.
Stearns; Stearns-Knight, 1899-1930, Cleveland.
Stevens-Duryea, 1902-27, Chicopee Falls, Mass.
Studebaker, 1902-64, South Bend, Ind.
Stutz, 1911-35, Indianapolis.
Thomas, 1902-19, Buffalo.
Tucker, 1946-48, Chicago.
Tulsa, 1917-23, Tulsa, Okla.
Velie, 1909-28, Moline, Ill.
Viking, 1929-30, Lansing.
Wayne, 1904-08, Detroit.
White, 1900-18, Cleveland.
Willys; Willys-Overland; Willys-Knight, 1903-63, Terre Haute, Ind.; Indianapolis; Toledo.
Winton, 1897-24, Cleveland.

YUGOSLAVIA
Zastava, 1954-present, Kragujevac.

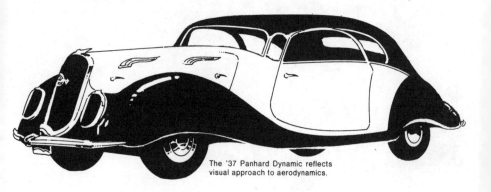

The '37 Panhard Dynamic reflects visual approach to aerodynamics.

Index